LIFE IN PIECES

finding beauty in the ashes

JODI O. SAPPE

LIFE IN PIECES:
Finding Beauty in the Ashes
Jodi O. Sappe

ISBN (Print Edition): 9781667807973
ISBN (eBook Edition): 9781667807980

I dedicate this book to two of my greatest blessings, Lawson & Bella. Your courage, strength, & resilience make me so proud. I love you.

To Jason Fuller, you left this world too soon and will always have a special place in our hearts. You were my only link to my husband for ten months & you didn't have to be as kind and gracious as you were. You encouraged me, celebrated with me, and you envisioned what has now come to pass. If only you could be here to see it. We love you, Fuller!

TABLE OF CONTENTS

FOREWORD

God knew what He was doing when He saved Brad and Jodi Sappe from the plans of the enemy. I first met Jodi and Brad in 2013 at a residential ministry program for men called No Longer Bound. Brad and my brother Charley were in the program together due to their addiction and cycle of self-destruction. On Saturdays, the immediate family could visit with their loved one allowing those of us who came regularly to form a special bond. It was a time of great uncertainty for all of us as the thought of would our loved one kick this addiction that was destroying not only their lives but also the lives of their family who somehow still held on to a glimmer of hope.

That was eight years ago and since then I have had the honor of witnessing miracle after miracle in the restoration of this beautiful family. God didn't just save Brad's life through this program, but his entire family was healed and restored in the process and then they set out to make a difference in the lives of other men who are battling addiction and to help the family heal.

The book you hold in your hand is a book of God's Redeeming Love, Amazing Grace, and His Power to Restore. It's a story of a family that was shattered into pieces but how God took those broken pieces and created something Beautiful!

Lisa Hensley

Katlyn's Promise Ministries

Jackson, Ga.

CHAPTER 1
The Foundation

"You wanna go to the prom with me?" I had no idea the level of intensity that question held. At the time, I was a 16-year-old socialite who just needed to get to all the proms. I knew this guy because we were from the same county, which included a few small towns, and his best friend happened to be the brother of one of my best friends. We both played ball at the local rec-league, so we ran in some of the same circles, but I didn't know him well and really thought he was kind of cocky. However, I wanted to go to that school's prom and he was my ticket, so I said yes. Little did I know, I would continue to say yes to him for the next 20+ years.

This is my story. A story of love, loss, restoration, and redemption. There is plenty of grace, humor, and forgiveness sprinkled in too for good measure.

Currently, as a nation we find ourselves in a drug epidemic, so I write this book, hoping that I can shed light on a dark place and give hope to the hopeless. God has done amazing things in my life and in the life of my husband, but to experience the amazing, suffering had to come first. I have been told that you must go through the pain before you can get to the other side and experience victory. I am forever grateful that Jesus took us through the mud and the muck, because without getting dirty along the way, we would not have cleaned up so well. The valleys and the pits are where growth happens, not by our own strength, but in His. If you find yourself in a pit or a valley today, take heart because Jesus is there with you and promises to walk with you. Take his hand and trudge through until you get to the other side. I promise there IS another side and it has a much better view.

There have been so many times in my life that the hand of Jesus has been so evident, and I feel so fortunate to be able to say that as I take inventory of my last 40 years. I am going to start this story in the most appropriate place, which of course is the beginning.

I was born on June 22, 1979, to Billy and Sheryl Turner Outler. My mom's first cousin was in labor that same day and by God's providence, my cousin, Jennifer, and I share the same birthday. We were even born in the same hospital just hours apart. Our grandparents were the best of friends (brothers who married girls that were BFFs), and they each got to welcome their first grandchild together on the same day. As you can imagine, Jenn and I were spoiled rotten.

I went home from the hospital with my parents to our little town tucked in the heart of Georgia where Momma and Daddy would raise me as an only child until my sister came along in 1987. I grew up in church so Sunday School, worship services, GA's and Acteens were all I had ever known. (Shout out to all the girls who grew up Southern Baptist) I am forever grateful for the strong foundation in my life that began when I was a kid. I had a typical childhood filled with summers playing ball, swimming, and hanging out with friends and family.

I had my first boyfriend in the eighth grade and when that ended, I casually dated different guys through my junior year of high school. I was all about the social scene so homecoming, sporting events, dances, or anything that required gathering with others in a cute outfit was my jam. I enjoyed being with people and I loved being with my friends. At the end of my junior year, just a few months shy of my 17th birthday, I started dating the boy who would eventually become my husband. I learned that those kinds of stories really do happen, and now that my kids are in their teens, I sometimes wonder if they have already crossed paths with their future spouses.

As I mentioned, I had known this boy most of my life since we lived in the same area. There were two private schools in the neighboring town, I went to one and he went to the other. Since I loved going to all the things, attending the other school's prom was always a must. This year (circa 1996), my guy friends at the other school were all in relationships, so I wasn't sure how I was going to get myself to that JMA prom. Then Brad Sappe called. Game over.

There was no fluff or chit chat, he just said, "So do you want to go to the prom with me?" and I said, "I guess." So the date was set and when April rolled around, we went. He was a gentleman and we actually had a good time together, so we decided to go on another date, then another, and then I started going to his baseball games and before we knew it, we were "going steady." One night we were on Highway 57 on the way home from a date, and I don't remember all the details, but I remember that ride because there was a moment in that truck when my heart and brain connected, and I knew I was in love with him. (In full disclosure, it probably helped that he had just bought me some new clothes from my favorite store – he was speaking my love language long before we even knew there were love languages.) Seriously though, he reached out to hold my hand as he drove us down that main road and it felt like his hand was made to hold mine. I knew I was in love and I was smitten.

We continued to date through high school and then I went off to college a few hours away, while he opted to stay back and attend the local college. Of course, I was most excited about living on my own and going through rush (now called recruitment) so I could pledge my loyalty to a sorority. I became a proud Kappa Delta and enjoyed myself to the fullest in those years. Brad was also enjoying himself back at the local college. He did not participate in Greek life, so he didn't understand my social calendar and a little space grew between us as I did my thing and he did his. We even broke up for a season. His good looks coupled with his athleticism and charm definitely got him noticed around the GCSU campus. When I would go home to visit, and we would go out and a pretty girl spoke to him, I'd ask, "How do you know her?" and he would smile that crooked smile and say, "I had class with her." At the time I didn't find it amusing but as we aged, it became a running joke. Somehow, he had class with ALL the pretty girls.

Brad and I were young and living life to the fullest until we experienced our first tragedy as a couple. The date was March 8, 2000. I was 20 and Brad was 21. Brad's daddy was a lifelong resident of our county and a local business owner of a HVAC company known appropriately as Sappe's Heating & Air. On that fateful day, he was out checking on a crew who was installing a new unit at the home of an elderly woman. No one knew at the time, but the glue that was being used on the ductwork was flammable so when Brad's daddy arrived at the job and turned on the unit, it ignited, and everything went up in flames.

CHAPTER 2
Life & Death

Brad's daddy, Mr. Larry, was standing in the hallway beside the floor furnace and as flames shot out, he reflexively began trying to put out the fire and in doing so, he lost his balance and fell into the fiery pit. He was able to get out and rescue crews arrived to get him to the hospital, but the local ER crew knew immediately they had to get him to the Burn Center for the best and most intensive care.

Just an hour before the accident, Mr. Larry had dropped by Brad's college apartment and brought some groceries and even chit chatted with his son. Neither could have known that would be their last conversation.

Mr. Larry was transported to the Augusta Burn Center, where he lived for five days before succumbing to his injuries. He was badly injured, but his death still came as a surprise because even though he had third-degree burns over a portion of his body, they said it would be a long road but he would recover. We had no reason to believe otherwise. Then on March 13, 2000, when they were preparing to do skin grafts, they moved him from his bed to the operating table but he went into cardiac arrest and died immediately.

It was such a tragic loss and a lot for a 21-year-old college kid to handle. Brad was making plans for his future when the rug was swept out from under him. That was the day we experienced firsthand that life can change in an instant. Brad and I had experienced other tragedies and lost people separately, but this was our first tragedy as a couple.

Brad was heartbroken but was strong and determined to keep going and to make his Daddy proud. He withdrew from school and got his state license in heating and air so that he could help run his Daddy's business and keep all the wheels turning. As the days and weeks passed, emotion and unresolved grief were put aside as he continued to go through the motions of daily life.

Before his Dad passed away, while he was still unconscious in ICU, Brad made all kinds of promises that he could never keep. He told his Dad that he would always stay in the family business, he was going to make him proud, take care of his Momma, and never let him down. Then months later when reality set in, he knew he would never be able to keep all those promises, and he felt shame and guilt. He shared with me that he could distinctly remember how lost he felt after funeral services. On the way to see a friend, he stopped on a back road because he was absolutely overwhelmed with the loss and grief of it all. For the first time, he truly realized that life as he knew it would never be the same again. His world had been turned upside down. He asked himself, "What in the world do I do now?" Little did we know that he would be asking that same question of himself for the next 15 years.

From my perspective, Brad was doing well. He had moments of grief but mostly he was just barreling forward. At the time, I didn't know much about counseling, but I knew enough to know that he and his family should get some. They didn't choose to, but again in my 20-year-old mind, Brad seemed to be doing okay. He even went through a period when he wouldn't even drink socially while with friends or at events, so I thought he was processing it well and as I said, I didn't yet know the benefit of counseling myseelf, so I didn't push the issue when it came up. We went on with our lives, checking on his Mom often, and him working full time in the family business alongside his mother and brother. What could possibly go wrong?

CHAPTER 3 – BRAD'S WORDS
Goodbye to my Hero

When my Dad died, I was an angry kid who was hurting but I had no idea how to ask for help. I spent my whole life thinking that men are tough, they don't show emotions. We pull ourselves up by our bootstraps and press on. That way of thinking almost cost me my life.

I have always been the kind of person that pushes forward. I will work and push through things and then after I am on the other side, I would realize the toll it had taken on me. So, when my Dad was in the hospital, I wouldn't allow myself to think about the fact that he may not survive. I was more concerned with his numbers, what the machines said, all the data and information because I didn't know how to feel emotion. I remember being so angry when he was in the hospital that I couldn't even pray. In a way, I blamed God. That is something that I would eventually have a hard time forgiving myself for. One of the most frustrating things that happens when you lose a loved one is that you have to watch everyone else's life return to normal in a matter of days but you know that yours never will. That is why I felt so overwhelmed when I drove by myself for that first time after Dad's death.

I did what I knew how to do – stuff it down and go to work every day. I was in no way ready to let go of my Dad so I thought the next best thing was to continue working in the company that he had built. For a short period of time my Dad's death revealed to me how short life really is. I stopped even drinking socially because I realized that drinking numbed the pain and I could not stop at one or two. But I later traded the alcohol for pain pills, they were much more discreet, and they worked just as well if not better than alcohol. I could hide pills in my pocket a lot easier than I could hide alcohol on my breath.

Brad and his Dad

CHAPTER 4

Young Love

The first journal I have a record of was started right after Brad proposed. I journaled all through our engagement and gave it to him on our wedding day, July 20, 2002. Parts of this book will be actual written records of the Lord's faithfulness in my life. Hope you find encouragement along the way and most of all, I hope that you recognize the power of our mighty God.

On December 21, 2001, Brad proposed to me. It was a perfect proposal at one of our favorite places and shortly after we (or I) started planning our wedding! The date was set for July and I couldn't wait for all the showers, parties, and of course the big day! I was on Cloud Nine or what some might call La La Land.

I am a type "A" personality. I always have a plan and I stick to it. I also LOVE to make a list. The joy and satisfaction I get from checking items off my list is unparalleled. It is no surprise then that I have always enjoyed writing and journaling my thoughts. I have found it to be cathartic over the years and during hard times it has truly been a lifeline. Now, I encourage everyone to journal because as I look back over my journals from the last 18 years, they are sweet reminders of God's faithfulness. I love that I have a written record of answered prayers. I have always said that I was going to publish some of my journal entries one day so the next several chapters will be actual entries from my journals. The ones I chose are some of my favorites because you can hear my desperation, you hear my cries to God, and then you see God respond. Some of these entries are favorites just for their sheer rawness. My journaling has evolved over the years and now it is more of a conversation between me and the Lord but in the beginning, I had my head in the clouds and thought I was living a fairytale. My early entries showcase a young, naïve girl who was head over heels in love and planning her perfect life complete with a picket fence, two kids, and a dog. That girl leaned in and started to grow spiritually just because she thought she was supposed to during the newlywed stage of life. When she faced her first hard thing, she realized that God had been there all along and had been preparing her for this marathon that was going to span ten plus years.

Journal Entry dated December 21, 2001

"I am on cloud nine! Brad proposed to me! He has been telling me over the last few weeks to make sure I am available the weekend of December 21st because he was playing in a golf tournament at Callaway Gardens and wanted me to come along. Seemed normal enough so I fell for it hook, line, and sinker. We had dinner at a really nice restaurant on the property and then we needed to run back to the cottage to grab our coats before going to see the Christmas lights. Brad opened the door to the cabin, I walked in first and there were a dozen red roses sitting on the table with a note that simply read "turn around" and when I did, Brad was on his knee with a grin on his face and a ring in his hand. He said, "Will you marry me?" and I exclaimed "YES!" after asking if he was serious. He said, "Do I look like I'm serious?" I cried and hugged him and then ran to call my Mom and my grandmother but they knew it was happening because Brad had already talked to my Daddy the previous week and asked for my hand. I was so excited!"

Journal Entry dated December 22, 2001 (middle of the night)

"Brad is snoozing away but I can't sleep a wink because I am still so excited! A million thoughts are running through my mind. I had not been able to get in touch with anyone except my family and Brad's mom. I got Ashley's voicemail and I got B's voicemail. I needed to talk to them and spread my good news but it seemed that it would have to wait until tomorrow."

Saturday, December 22, 2001

"We had a great breakfast and spent the day in the town over in LaGrange. Brad took me to get my nails done and we bought a couple of

Christmas gifts and then went back to the little village near our cottage where we had lunch and shopped. It was a wonderful day and I was still floating on air. It was an irreplaceable feeling that I wish I could put it in a bottle to drink every day for the rest of my life. We relaxed at our cottage that afternoon and then went out to dinner and rode the trolley through the Fantasy of Lights. We watched the kids in front of us and thought of how in a few years we could have a kid of our own. It was wonderful, and we are so excited about our future! This is the greatest Christmas season ever!"

Sidenote: I continued to journal and write super mushy lines about how in love I was. I will spare you from that but one line actually said "we were so in love that we seemed invincible." If only that had been true. It is so good to look back on the days when we were young and light-hearted. We had the world by the tail and so much light ahead of us.

CHAPTER 5

The Slippery Slope of poor decisions

February 16, 2002, rolled around, and we were just five months shy of our wedding date. On that fateful evening, Brad and I were involved in a car accident. It was a bad accident and there is no earthly explanation for why or how I survived it. We were young and had been out celebrating and drinking with friends. We started at a Mexican restaurant and then moved to a friend's apartment and ended the night downstairs at the bar. For some reason, Brad and I decided to leave before closing time and we got into my SUV and headed back towards Brad's house which was over 20 miles away.

We did not make it far. As we rounded a curve just past the local Dairy Queen, Brad lost control of the vehicle and we hit a power pole, took out a few columns on the porch (of a thankfully vacated home), flipped and the car rolled down a ravine. At some point during all of that I was ejected and flew out of the car exiting from the rear windshield. My body was lying in the middle of a main road. I literally landed right on the yellow lines. When we hit the power pole, the power in that area of town went out and this was roughly 1:30 a.m. so most people were asleep and wouldn't have noticed. However, there just happened to be a police officer from a neighboring county on a nearby road. He heard the commotion and saw the lights go out. By God's grace, this police officer (ironically named Brad) was the first person on the scene and the first person to see my body. He called me in as a fatality because I appeared dead and he could not find a pulse. A neighbor ran out of her house and the officer later told us that he said, "I here by deputize you – stand here with this girl while I search for the other victims." He found Brad sitting a few houses down clutching his arm but otherwise unscathed. The ambulance came and when they arrived, they found a faint pulse, so they loaded me up and took me to the local hospital. It was a terrible idea to drink and drive, one of 100's of bad decisions we had made but God can redeem really bad choices. I was learning that's one of his specialties.

All of the details of the accident have been shared with me as I have no memory of that night other than being at dinner and I can remember being in our friend's apartment and going to the bar. My Mom said that she and Daddy were called around 3:30 in the morning. By the time Mom, Dad, and my little sister arrived at the hospital it was a startling scene. She said the lawn and halls were filled with our friends. A few of our friends were in law enforcement, so when word got back to the bar about an accident and our friends couldn't locate us, they knew who was involved. Then my soon-to-be brother-in-law met Mom at the door of the hospital sobbing, saying he was so sorry. When Mom and Dad finally got back to me, I was on a table with a sheet pulled all the way to my chin, so they thought I was dead. The doctor told them I was still breathing but that my feet and hands were beginning to turn inward which is a sure sign of brain injury. They went on to say that they were not equipped to handle my injuries and that they needed to transport me to the nearest level 1 Trauma hospital. Thankfully, there is a world-class trauma hospital just forty-five minutes away in the next town.

I was intubated and loaded into the ambulance for transport. I was admitted to the new hospital (still unconscious) and moved to the neuro floor for tests and monitoring. The afternoon of my arrival, I just suddenly woke up. After all that, I opened my eyes (no longer intubated) and spoke! I was scratched and bruised but had no broken bones. I had a concussion but no other brain injury. I am just going to pause there so you can take that in. A girl who was ejected from a vehicle and originally had no pulse was absolutely fine. It as a miracle. I woke up, looked at my Mom and asked, "Can I walk?" Mom was stunned that I was awake and asking a logical question but she answered and said, "I don't know yet" then my second question was "Where is Brad?" She told me he was okay, was at home with his Mom and would visit soon.

I was only in the hospital for a few days and I did not require any rehab or physical therapy, but I did do a follow up at the Shepherd's Clinic in Atlanta. The Shepherd's Clinic is a hospital that specializes in medical treatment, research, and rehabilitation for people with spinal cord injury, brain injury, stroke, multiple sclerosis, and other neuromuscular conditions. It was the pinnacle of all the hospitals and those who were severely injured went there for help. I was referred for just one appointment to get a second opinion on my concussion and the effects of it. I don't think I truly knew how fortunate I was until that day. I was the only patient that "walked" through the entrance of that hospital. It was quite humbling, and I knew things could have gone much differently for me. I was not myself again until a month or so after the accident. Since my concussion had been severe and I had never been on such strong medication, I was literally out of my head until the middle of March. I had no real physical injuries. I was sore and a little beat up but mostly I was a walking, talking miracle of God and so was Brad. The doctor at Shepherd's Clinic agreed that I would be fine and that my brain would heal and I would only have some minor memory loss. It was evident to me that God left us here for a reason and we needed that wake up call to get back to where we needed to be spiritually. Brad never left my side during my recovery, we stayed with my parents some and with his Mom some. He was great and I could not have asked for more. We grew so much closer together, and we were so glad the accident happened because we realized once again how precious life is and how there is so much to life than partying with friends. Now, we just wanted to spend time with each other, family, and friends. We loved our church and were so excited to have a church home and be marrying each other. God put us together for a reason. We knew he must have a solid plan for us.

I was okay. I was more than okay, I had been saved, I had been spared from death and I knew it. I knew God had a purpose for me and my purpose was not yet completed so He saved me from death that night, healed me from what should have been serious injuries, and He clearly left me here for a reason. I had a slow recovery but was soon feeling like myself again and in July, I held my Daddy's arm as I walked down the aisle to my forever love.

CHAPTER 6 — BY BRAD

The Accident

On the afternoon of February 16, 2002, I looked at some documents from the burn center regarding my Dad's death. I read detailed documents and saw several vivid pictures of my Dad after his accident. The pain was more than I could bear so I started drinking that afternoon.

Jodi and I met up with some friends at a Mexican restaurant and then went downtown to a friend's bar. I don't remember much of the evening, but I do remember being inside the vehicle and having a sense of losing control because the vehicle was airborne. The next thing I remember is waking up in an upside-down vehicle. My arm was bent through the steering wheel and I was lying across the dash. I remember initially thinking that this must not be my time to die because the truth was, I hadn't really wanted to live since I lost my Dad.

I was transported to the hospital and I remember standing over Jodi's body while they were trying to put a tube in her mouth so they could transport her to the trauma hospital. I was being told that she would probably die and if she did live, she would most likely be a vegetable for the rest of her life. My world was turned upside again and I remember thinking that if it was true that God never puts more on you than you can handle then I was about to find out because I knew I couldn't handle losing her.

The next day, I woke up in my old bedroom at my Mom's house. I walked into the living room and I asked my older brother if Jodi was going to be okay. He looked at me with tears in his eyes and said, "No, she's not. She is at the trauma hospital now because they think she has brain and spinal injuries." All I knew to do was call a buddy to take me to the hospital so I could face whatever was before me. I prayed a lot on that 30 minute drive. When I got to the hospital and walked down the hallway, the first person I saw was Jodi's dad. I put on the bravest face I had and told him I was so sorry. To my utter amazement, he looked at me and said, "I don't want to hear that. She chose to get in the car with you so it is not all your fault." I have always known what a good man her Daddy was but that day he reached Saint status in my eyes. I walked in the room and to my surprise, Jodi was awake. She looked at me and said, "Why are you wearing the same thing you had on yesterday? What's up Re-run?" I knew she was going to be okay. After a couple more days in the hospital it was apparent that we were witnessing a miracle. Despite all the doctor's reports, Jodi was going to be okay. I would later joke that she wasn't really okay because she still wanted to marry me in July. I will never forget how close my life came to changing forever that day. After the accident I watched Jodi's life drastically change as she grew closer and closer to the Lord. She knew she had been given a second chance and was not going to waste it. I knew I had also been given a second chance, but it would be years before I could forgive myself for the position I had put her in. I could care less that I had almost killed myself, but I had a hard time coming to grips with the fact that I almost killed my future bride.

CHAPTER 7
Newlywed Bliss

Friday, July 19, 2002 Journal Entry

"I can't believe I am getting ready for my bridal luncheon! I have not been nervous all along but this morning I woke up at 7 a.m. and could not get back to sleep! I had butterflies and I was emotional. I got teary-eyed each time I spoke and then I calmed down. Mom, Daddy, Sister and I sat around and we laughed and we talked. Dad and I practiced dancing and we all got a good laugh out of him. He propped his hand on my head and then Mom tried on her wedding shoes and she and Daddy danced too. It was such a special morning and I will always cherish that morning with them. I can't wait for the wedding – it is gonna be a great weekend!"

Our Wedding Day, July 20th, 2002

August 24, 2002

"It has been an awful long time since I've written but married life has kept me busy! This has been amazing and Brad and I are so happy! Other people are always commenting on how happy we are and I know that means our love is strong enough to touch those around us. It is so much fun to be married and to never have to leave him at night to go back to Mom and Dad's. I love planning meals and entertaining. We have already hosted several guests for dinner, and it has been so much fun. One night we tricked Mom into eating deer meat and another time I had a big layered cake fail. Brad has been the most wonderful husband. He was always a good boyfriend but this job suits him to a "T"! He has said the most touching things to me. On our wedding night he shared that he had not felt happiness like this since losing his Dad. That meant the world to me that I could make him feel that way. We start teaching a Sunday School class tomorrow at church. The Walkers (ages 9-12 months) and I am so excited and grateful that we can grow in our relationship with God this way as we serve. I can't wait to see what He has in store for us!"

Side note: I love how excited I am about everything having no idea what God has in store and thank goodness we never do or we might not keep going.

CHAPTER 8
The Foundation

I know now that God was beginning to prepare our hearts and build the foundation that would support us in all the years ahead.

October 9, 2002

"Brad and I started a bible study together. It is on Ephesians 4. I have listed some key points below:

- Don't allow petty differences to dissolve Christian unity
- Pray for people whose actions or personalities get on your nerves and spend some time getting to know them better
- No one is beyond God's reach (I would need to commit this one to memory)
- Be forgiving (and this one too)

We were enjoying married life and in March of 2003, Brad tore his ACL while playing football in an adult league. The injury required surgery, physical therapy, and pain pills. Typical stuff and I did not think much of it. That summer, I took a mission trip to Peru – Brad was supposed to go too but because of his knee injury and all that would be involved in the trip, his doctor did not allow him to go. While I was away, Brad used the wedding journal I had given him to record his own thoughts."

From Brad's journal page:

"I just finished folding clothes and I thought I'd tell you that I left out all of your clothes except a tee shirt and pajama shorts because I didn't want to mess anything up. I was telling friends how weird it is that you have rubbed off on me. Like keeping the house neat and clean is one thing, but last night

I had to get up and close all the blinds. I never used to worry about stuff like that but here I am, and I opened them all again this morning. I also found myself turning on all the lamps like you do at night. Oh well, I love you and can't wait to see you."

In July just before our one-year anniversary, Brad came to me and said he had been abusing his pain medication but that now it was under control and he was going to stop. I was like "okay! Thanks for telling me!" Brad has always been an adrenaline junkie and has never really been afraid of anything. I knew he liked to take risks and I knew he had experimented with drugs in college. I also knew he was an all or nothing kind of guy but none of that came to mind upon his confession. So, we went on our weekend anniversary trip to the coast and had a great time. Time rolled on and Brad was regularly hanging out with some people I was not incredibly fond of and we had some arguments about time he spent with them. I just had a bad feeling in my gut. They always seemed to be working on cars, riding four wheelers, or playing softball. All those things were in fact happening but as I would soon find out, there was much more happening at those gatherings.

Fast forward to the fall of 2004. In August, we found out we were expecting our first child and we were over the moon! We had not been trying for too long and we were so excited to become parents and meet our first little bundle of joy.

In October of 2004, I came home one evening from teaching a workout class in town and I decided to check my email. Brad was not home at the time and as I sat down at the computer and hit the space bar, a screen popped up that Brad haphazardly forgot to close out before leaving home. The screen showed confirmation for an order of pills. Brad had long since recovered from his knee injury and those prescriptions had run out, so he was now ordering from a pill mill online and having the goods delivered to a friend's house. One of the friends I previously mentioned that didn't exactly give me the warm fuzzies. I was floored. I didn't know what they had been up to but I never would have guessed it was drugs. I didn't know what to do. My mind raced with all that was happening. I knew that I couldn't call my parents because Brad and I were newlyweds and I didn't want to bring them into this. I had heard enough about how you don't tell your parents all the details of your marriage so I felt like I was in this new season but who could I call? I ended up calling Brad's mother and older brother. I asked them to come over for an intervention. They came right over and we waited on Brad to get home. He finally came in and we were all sitting in our living room waiting on him. He said "What are ya'll doing?" and then it began. I don't remember all the words, but he admitted what he had been doing and that he had a problem. He agreed to go for treatment. We knew nothing about addiction or treatment centers, so I called the crisis line at a local hospital and I made plans to take him the following week. He was checked into the hospital to be detoxed so he resided at the hospital for two weeks and then came home and went back daily for a partial day program. I was sad and lonely while he was away, but I never felt hopeless. I really thought he was cured when he came back home and that we would never face this battle again.

Detox sounded like a serious word so surely to goodness he was healed, and we were going to be fine. We celebrated Thanksgiving and Christmas, winter changed to spring and we prepared to welcome our baby boy, Lawson, into the world.

Lawson arrived on May 25, 2005 at 5:25 p.m. We should have played the lottery in 5's that day. Life rocked along and we figured out how to be parents. I remember leaving the hospital three days after Law was born and everything looked different like literally. The world outside my car window looked different and there was this newborn baby strapped in a car seat as I held his little hand all the way home. I really couldn't believe that the hospital let him leave with us. We didn't know how to do this. But like all new parents, we figured it out by trial and error and as I write this our son is fifteen, so we have kept him alive and that is a lot more than I can say for any plant I have ever tried to raise.

Brad's words about his first Detox Experience:

"I had no idea what to expect on my first trip to detox. I knew I had a problem and I knew I couldn't stop so I was willing to give it a shot. I remember feeling sick, remorseful and like a failure. The Detox center was full of other addicts as well as mental health patients and I had never experienced anything like that in my life. I had no idea how comfortable I would eventually become in that setting. For two weeks I was tapered off alcohol and opiates and my days were filled with group meetings and crafts. I thought I was doing well, and I really thought I was going to be okay when I left. I don't remember worrying about if I could stay clean, but I do remember being afraid of what everyone from my hometown would think of me."

When Lawson turned a year old in May of 2006, we decided we needed a fresh start. So, we moved out of our first home, and bought a new house about 30 miles away from our hometown and our family. In June we moved into our new home. Things seemed to be rocking along fine but then just a month after our move it was clear that Brad had fallen off the wagon. The signs were all there. He was sweaty most of the time, he would nod off while sitting, and he was on his phone all the time.

We knew he had to be detoxed again and this time he would need more than just a detox. He needed something that packed a little more punch like a long-term rehab. We found out about a program called Penfield in Union Point, Georgia and made plans for him to go. He was detoxed at the same hospital as before and when a bed opened up at Penfield, we took it. Beds were not often open at Penfield (there was usually a waiting list) but by the grace of God, one bed became open the exact day Brad was discharged from the hospital, so he was able to go straight there with no gap in between treatment.

I vividly remember that drive from our home to Union Point. My best friend, Bethany was our driver and we traveled in her car. Brad was quiet most of the way there. He was willing to go because deep down he knew he needed help, but he was not buying into the six-week program and was a little perturbed at me for deciding this was the plan. We said our goodbyes and he was not happy that I was actually leaving him there, but I left anyway because I knew he needed help.

As Bethany and I drove away, Brad was sitting on top of a picnic bench with his head hanging. It was a pitiful scene and one that is forever etched into my memory. I felt so sorry for him and I felt so sorry for myself. As any good friend would, Bethany anticipated the ride home might be rough, so she purchased a big bag of chocolates and as we rode along we stuffed our faces with chocolate goodness in an effort to soothe our broken hearts.

CHAPTER 9
Rehab, Take 1

A s I mentioned, Penfield is a six-week program and for the first two weeks there are no calls, letters, or visits. I was still a relatively new Mom, in a new home with my one-year-old and not terribly far away from family but much farther than I used to be. It was a scary time and I was lonely and ashamed. I thought "I need some help and I need some prayers but who can I tell?" I immediately thought of my Sunday School class and then the very next thought was "I certainly can't tell them!" and I will never forget where I was in that moment because it was like God hit me over the head with a ton of bricks. I was driving down Forest Hill Road and I felt God clearly say to me "If you can't tell your Sunday School class then *who* can you tell?!?!" and I thought that is exactly right God, good point!

So, I made plans to share what was going on that very next Sunday. I had many friends and family that would come and stay with Law and I, while Brad was away and on this particular weekend, my cousin, Greg, who was like a little brother to m volunteered. Greg was also an electrician by trade so he offered to hang some of my light fixtures. Greg went to church with me the next morning. We dropped Law off in the nursery and made our way to the Sunday School room. I had already been talking with two of my best friends, Katherine and Mary and they knew what I was going to share. I knew that I likely could not get through the news without dissolving into tears, so I wrote my words down just in case. That way, the words could be passed off to Mary or Kat if needed. We had an extended fellowship time that morning and I made small talk just like the others and then the class leader asked if there were any prayer requests. I raised my hand as I silently prayed "Lord, prepare their hearts for this" and as I began to talk, my voice began to shake and I handed the paper to Mary who spoke the rest of my words for me. Mary talked as Kat held my hand. As Mary finished, the class leader said that we were going to spend the rest of our class time praying over my situation.

It was a defining moment in the life of that Sunday School class. I sat and cried quietly as people gathered around me, laid hands on me, and prayed for me, for Lawson, and for Brad. To this day, it is one of the most precious memories of my life. In the coming weeks, the sweet people of that class became the hands and feet of Jesus as they brought meals, ran errands, or babysat Lawson. Some of the men took care of our yard and it was all just precious. There was one couple in particular that we had seen around but had not gotten to know very well and after I shared that day, he came up to me and said he had a cousin that struggled with addiction and asked how he could help. That man's name was Paul and during that time a friendship was born and to this day, Paul and his wife, Gina are some of our dearest friends. We may have never gotten to know them if not for that heartbreaking day. God is always working behind the scenes for your good and His glory, friend.

It was sometime during that six-week term at Penfield that I had what I call my first God experience. I clearly heard God speak to my heart and He told me not to leave my marriage. It had not been on my mind too much at that point but there were some people in my life who had differing opinions. I began to believe that God called me to this life and maybe that is why I was saved in that car accident years ago, to be Brad's wife and help him through all of this. I viewed it as my lot in life, I was called to be the wife of an addict.

After the first two weeks I got to visit Brad at Penfield on Saturdays and we even got to have conjugal visits like people in prison do. I would pick him up and we'd go rent a hotel room for a few hours and do what God intended for man and woman to do. It was surreal. I mean who rents a hotel room for a few hours at the time? The answer is people who are having affairs, prostitutes, and married men who are in rehab.

If you have never visited a rehab, you are really missing an experience. Some are like what you see on TV and some are not like that at all. Penfield sort of reminded me of the place where Sandra Bullock dried out that movie

"28 days." I learned that you may dry out in 28 days, but you are far from healed in that short time frame.

Brad completed the Penfield program with flying colors and came back to us. Penfield is a faith-based program so when he returned home, he was on fire for the Lord. He wanted to serve in ALL the places at church, do bible studies, and rededicate his life by being baptized again. He had seen the light and this time I just knew we were healed!

I had never been to support groups or group meetings and I was not ready to start but the folks at Penfield suggested that I go to something called Alanon. Alanon is a twelve-step program that is designed for family and loved ones of alcoholics and addicts. I did not want to go. I will never forget that first meeting and how I awkwardly walked in and kept my head down for most of the hour. I did not want to be there, and I blamed Brad for everything. As much as I dreaded those meetings, they began to grow on me over time. I even began looking forward to them. If nothing else I looked forward to them because I knew exactly what was going to happen for that one hour each day. After living in such chaos that was so comforting to me. The people in those rooms began to grow on me too and I got a sponsor and began working the steps. Alanon taught me to keep the focus on myself, own my part in everything, and to not let Brad's behavior control mine. There is something inherently comforting about being with a group of people who are walking or have walked the same path. It is like any other support group, I guess, because we all feel more comfortable when we share with someone who actually gets what we are going through.

It was in Alanon that I made one of the dearest friends of my life. She and I ran in the same circles, had some mutual friends, and were in Junior League together. Heck, our boys even went to the same daycare but our paths rarely crossed at any of those places. Then one night, as I sat in the big group circle at my meeting, she walked in. She looked a lot like I did my first time – a little green, a little timid, and a lot ashamed. As usual, I shared some of my words and thoughts during the meeting. Afterwards, she came up to me to officially introduce herself and told me that what I had shared that night was exactly what she needed to hear. A bond was formed in that room that night and 12 years later our friendship is one of the rarest and most precious gifts of my life. Our boys are the same age, her husband also found healing and new life of freedom & now our husbands are big buddies too. Only God could orchestrate all that. So thankful.

CHAPTER 10
The Stork comes again...

In 2007, we found out we were expecting our second child, a sweet baby girl. She would also be a May baby like our son. On May 14, 2008, Bella Grace entered our world and it has never been the same. We were over the moon and in love with our little princess! Bella was beautiful and healthy, Law was wild and free at three years old (and potty trained) so life was good! Until it wasn't.

We were settled in our home by now and I was on a twelve-week maternity leave from my banking career and Brad was doing okay or so I thought. Early in my leave, I realized something was off and my assumptions turned out to be true. He was using again. I knew that he had to go. I had to exhibit that tough love I kept hearing about, so I told him he had to leave, and we were separated that first summer of Bella's life. During those two months, he stayed in the country in a little hunting cabin that some of his family built. Nobody had to know because he knew how to get in there and it was back in the woods. The only way folks would find out if he was there was if they noticed the gate open and peered through the woods and saw his truck. One day, someone did just that and when word got back to his Mom, she invited him to come stay with her. He accepted. Of course, he did because that invitation meant someone to do his laundry, cook his meals, and a nice place to lay his head. That was really hard for me because I had just made the hardest, biggest tough love move of my life and now someone had intervened and offered him comfort so he still wasn't experiencing circumstances to the fullest. If you are wondering why we stopped at two kids, this is your answer. Brad did not tend to fare well after births, so I was not going to press my luck with a third.

This was the third time he had relapsed, and I was finally mad enough to make a move. Since I was still on maternity leave and mostly just at home taking care of the kids, nobody really knew we were separated because I wasn't going anywhere which again was normal with such a small baby. If I did go out, I could just make up an excuse about where Brad was and that is kind of how it went during the summer of 08'.

There was a point along the year that I re-visited a counselor that Brad and I had first seen back in 2004. She was a Christian counselor and I will never forget the day I left my newborn and three-year-old at home with a friend so I could meet with her and talk about our recent struggles. She looked right at me and said, "You need to divorce him" and that life with an addict would always be this way. She even gave me a few suggestions for divorce attorneys. I left her office so deflated I could barely breathe. It was just not what I expected to hear from her. Her word and instruction was something I greatly valued, and held her on such a high pedestal that typically whatever she said to do was the gospel for me. Thankfully, this time I didn't act on her instruction but instead got on my knees and continued to seek wise earthly counsel as well. The words of that counselor would sting for years to come.

Brad came home in August and not because everything was fine, or that I was even ready to be reconciled but because I was going to back to work and needed an extra set of hands. I thought even if he is high, he can at least hold a bottle or bathe a kid. I just needed some help around the house with the two little kids. It felt more like a roommate moving back in. He came back and tried to do better, and we began to forge a new life.

The year 2008 was a significant one because it brought us Bella but it was also the year I met the woman who would become one of my dearest confidants as well as my mentor for life. One of my best friends, Katherine, invited me to a bible study she was a part of and had been for a couple of years. They met at the home of a woman who had grown kids and was a few seasons ahead of all of us 30-somethings. I loved the idea of being led by someone like that and I also loved that this was a small, tight-knit group. Also, you were not invited to come unless you had experienced some hard circumstances. One woman was in a really difficult marriage, one was getting over cancer, two women were raising special needs kids, and a whole host of other issues were evident all across Vicki's beautiful living room. I was right at home. Looking back, if Kat had never invited me to the study, or if I had never agreed to go, I would have missed out on one of the most sacred relationships of my life. The woman who entered my life that year was called Vicki and later I met her husband, Charles and they both became major players in our lives.

I share all that to encourage you to pay attention to those holy spirit nudges you feel in your heart. Pay attention to unlikely meetings and be quick to act when you feel prompted to invite someone somewhere or to facilitate a meeting. Pay attention to the opportunities God presents to you because they could be life-changing for you or someone else.

The next years would send us in what seemed like a never-ending spiral of drug addiction. Brad visited several detoxes, partial day programs, etc. The years from 2009-11 were okay"ish" but the year 2012 in particular was a really hard one for us.

CHAPTER 11
A New Year, a New Disaster

Time marched on as it tends to and by 2012, he, and "we," hit rock bottom. I called one of my dearest friends at this point and asked her to hold me accountable to my promise because I told her if he used again, I was leaving. Katherine was the friend on the other end of the line that day and is that friend that I can say awful things to that I might not ever say to anyone else. She is also that friend who holds me accountable and speaks truth to me. If you don't have a friend like that, you need to get one. (free advice)

We went to counseling and Brad did what was required of him which was the norm and not unusual. Things were not good between us, but he was always remorseful and always more than willing to get help.

We made it through 2012 somehow and rang in a brand new year. It was 2013 and we had no idea what was in store for us. Buckle up friends, it's gonna get bumpy.

February of 2013 is when it all finally fell apart for us. Brad was a functional addict so he held it together a lot longer than most can. A functional addict is someone who can hide their addiction well. They don't miss a beat and they still show up and they do all the things you need them to do but they are just high while they do it.

Brad had a lot working in his favor as he was self-employed, had access to money, and had more than one co-dependent in his life. Someone was always there to catch him when he fell, and it is a fact that we don't learn without consequences. Here, is the timeline of events that led us to the breaking point.

February 5, 2013 – We had dinner as a family around the table and it seemed to be a normal Wednesday night. After dinner I was clearing the table and Brad was in the den, sitting in his recliner. I walked through the room and realized that he didn't look right and just then, before my eyes, he started seizing or having what I thought was a stroke. I called some friends to come sit with the kids so we could go to the hospital. Probably a year prior to this, I had to call an ambulance for a similar episode and we did an entire neuro work-up only to find he was abusing a substance; so this time, I decided to skip the ambulance bill and drive him myself.

They took him back immediately and did lots of tests. His history of addiction was included in his paperwork and I will never forget the ER doctor calling me out in the hallway and telling me that he had run every test he could think of and everything looked fine. He said he could almost guarantee that Brad had taken something that caused these symptoms. We got home around 4 a.m. and I slept right through my alarm, so we were both late for work the next day and our kids were late for school. I already felt like a failure and so shameful about my current life circumstances, and now my kids were late to elementary school?! I was the woman of the year. The enemy had a field day in my mind that morning. We all eventually got off to where we needed to be and started our days.

February 6, 2013 – After work, the kids did homework and I started dinner. It felt like a normal day at this point. It was nearing 6 p.m. and Brad was not home yet, which was unusual, so I called him up. He told me that he had put his four-wheeler in storage and was headed home. He didn't sound good and his speech was slurring. As time ticked by, I called again, and he said he was on Riverside Drive just a mile or so from our home. I told him I was going to stay on the phone with him until he arrived safely at home. I was standing on the walkway in our front yard watching for his truck. I watched as he swerved down the road and almost hit a car head on before wheeling in our driveway and taking out half the bushes on the edge of the yard.

I realized the car that he had swerved to miss was turning around to come back, so I ran down the driveway and instructed Brad to not get out of the truck. He was clearly high as a kite and smacking on candy like a five-year-old.

I walked back up the driveway and a near hysterical woman got out and shouted, "Was that your husband who almost hit me?" She went on to say that she was a mother and grandmother and that he could have taken her out. She asked, "Is he drunk?" I said, "No ma'am, he has been having seizures (which was partially true or so I thought) and I think he just had one in the car." I didn't miss a beat stepping up and covering up because that had become my norm. She quieted down when I brought up the seizures, got in her car and left. Next, I went back down to the truck to re-instruct Brad to stay put so I could go inside and get our kids (4- and 7-year-olds) situated in a way so they wouldn't have to see their Daddy in that condition. So much of our story is full of statements that include "only by the grace of God" and this was another one because any other day the kids would have heard him pull up and either run outside or have been waiting at the door. Brad was their hero, the fun parent. There is never anything quite like a Daddy coming home.

I got the kids busy in their rooms and told them to stay there, then I went and got Brad out of the truck. He could barely walk, and I knew this problem was out of control and could no longer be covered up. I got Brad to the bedroom where he all but passed out on the bed. Then I called our precious friends, Vicki and Charles and asked them to come pick up the kids. They fed them, bathed them and put them to bed at their house that night. After the kids were gone, I called Katherine, who also happens to be a pharmacist and I told her what was happening and I remember those next few moments so clearly. Kat said, "Go to the bedroom and make sure he is still breathing. I will wait on the phone but go make sure he is still alive." So, I put the phone down and all the way to our bedroom I thought to myself, "What if he is not breathing? That wouldn't be the end of the world, at least I would have closure and there would be finality." That sounds heartless I know but when you have experienced addiction for so many years, death seems merciful. I reached our room and leaned over his body. He was still breathing. I went back and reported to Kat and she said, "Good, you need to see if you can figure out what he has taken," so I went to his truck and searched. I found an empty pill bottle but of course the label was ripped off. I could tell it had been filled by our local pharmacy. Kat told me to call the pharmacy to see if they would tell me what was last filled for him. I called and in God's providence the Pharmacy Manager (whom we had gotten to know over the years and never answered the phone) answered the phone and I frantically told him what was happening and he gave me the prescription info. It was not even an opioid or something that one would normally get high on which showed me the progression of his disease, he was abusing anything he could get his hands on. Next, I walked inside to my big red chair and sobbed. I tried to make sense of the situation and I didn't know what to do but I knew I needed someone to come over and to come over now. So, I called my life long best friend, Bethany. You might remember that she is also the one who drove us to Penfield back in 2006.

I could write another book just on our friendship and things we have overcome together so she was my natural go to. We have been friends since we were children and her favorite story to tell is that there is a little bible that was a gift from my family to hers (I was born in June of 79' and she came along in November) so it said to Baby Miller from Baby Outler. All that to say, when I called, she came running. I filled her in and she asked, "What can I do?" Through my tears, I said, "Please call my parents." She did and they too came running.

It is a 30-minute drive for them so that gave us time to clean up my dining room table because it was covered with pictures and decorations for the surprise birthday party we were throwing that very weekend for my Dad and grandmother! We dumped everything in one of the kid's bedrooms and waited on my parents. They arrived with a look of worry and concern on their faces and we explained what was happening. By this point, Brad was awake and he came strutting out of the bedroom (wearing only his boxers) and said, "What are ya'll doing?" My Dad, always with a quick wit said, "I think the real question is what are **YOU** doing?" I ushered Brad back to bed and soon he began calling my cell from the house phone saying he was hungry and requesting a peanut butter and jelly sandwich. I could have strung him up by his toes.

I was in touch with the counselor we had been seeing for the last six months and he was guiding me and making recommendations. He suggested a real, long-term, residential rehab program called No Longer Bound. I said that sounded fine, I really didn't care where he went, but he had to get out of our home. There was a process for getting in NLB which was fine because he needed to detox first anyway. I let him sleep at our home that first night because he just needed to sleep it off and the next morning, I told him he had to go. Thankfully, our friends Vicki and Charles entered the picture again and offered to let him stay at their house until he could be admitted to the detox program. They loved our little family and had so much compassion for Brad so they felt like this was something they could do to help. I will never forget those days. Brad went to Charles and Vicki's home and then decided he should try to be detoxed locally so he had Charles drive him to the hospital. He was angry with Charles for some reason (a clue he was not in his right mind) and asked him to just leave him there. Charles didn't want to but Brad was persistent so eventually Charles left. All of this was happening while Bella and I were at school with my parents watching Lawson perform in the school talent show. The little fella was only in first grade and was performing a comedy act. The crowd loved him! I wanted to include this in the book because this is such a testament to the statement that you never know what people are dealing with because as people watched Lawson on that stage or saw us smiling in the audience, nobody would have ever guessed what we were dealing with at home or that we didn't even know where Brad was at the moment.

Meanwhile, Brad didn't get into the hospital, so he called Charles and asked him to come back and get him. Of course Charles did and for the next few days, Brad slept on Charles and Vicki's couch and in their guest bedroom. Vicki was talking with our counselor about getting him in the NLB program and she always talks about how she filled out the NLB application for him and then printed it for Brad to sign. Brad was so out of it that he signed crooked and it went half way up the page. Maybe that wonky signature helped him get in rehab sooner.

NLB (this is how I will refer to No Longer Bound from here on out) suggested that Brad detox in Atlanta at Anchor Hospital. After a few tumultuous days with Charles and Vicki, by the grace of God, he was notified that he would be admitted into NLB upon successful completion of the detox program. We would later learn this was a huge God wink because there was regularly a waiting list for people to enter NLB but Brad would be going straight in. Charles drove Brad to Anchor Hospital, checked him in and left him there. I will be forever grateful for the role Charles and Vicki played during this season of our lives.

CHAPTER 12

The Year that Changed Us Forever

Brad remained at Anchor until February 20th and now it was my turn to play taxi. I had not intended to go but when I talked to the NLB staff they encouraged me to come because they said regardless of what happened they were concerned about the whole family. They told me their mission was to rescue addicts, regenerate addicts, and restore families. I was intrigued and knew this program was unlike anything we had done before.

I was scheduled to pick Brad up at Anchor and take him to NLB the next morning. Our baby girl had started ballet the year before and her first recital was coming up. It was parent watch day that afternoon, so my Mom and I went because I had to leave straight from there for the hospital and Mom was taking over with the kids. I arrived at Anchor around 5:30 or 6 p.m. and it took a little while to check him out. We were spending the night in Atlanta so we could report to NLB the next day. Anchor Hospital is near the airport, so I made a reservation at an airport hotel and it just happened to be the Westin, the same hotel where we had spent our wedding night. Oh, the irony! We checked into the hotel and then went out to dinner. It was a solemn occasion and we could each feel the looming uncertainty of the future. You could have cut the tension with a knife. The next morning, we went to a nearby Wal-Mart to get the things he needed to take with him like towels, sheets, etc. Afterwards he had a steak lunch at Longhorn like it was his last meal and then we made the drive to NLB. It was February 21st and our interview was set for 1 p.m.

We walked into the front office and were ushered to a board room where Brad was given some paperwork to fill out. Two men entered the room; they looked like ex-military and spoke like it too. There was nothing warm and fuzzy about it all. Today, I can understand their methods but that day it was all super intimidating. They spoke to Brad directly, and harshly, and asked him questions like "Do you love your wife?" and of course Brad said he did and they retorted that they didn't believe him because he was not acting as if that statement were true. They called him out for being a business owner and thinking he was better than every other addict just because he had held it together a little longer and not lost as much. They told him "if" he was accepted, he would walk down that hill and encounter all kinds of men and that he was just like them because he too was an addict. They kept saying "if" he was accepted which made me squirm in my seat. When they walked out, I looked at Brad and said, "They keep saying IF you get in this program and I don't know where you are going if you don't get in because you are not coming back home with me." And for the first time in my life, I meant it. Shortly afterwards they came back and said he was in. Brad went to get his things out of the car while another staff member came in to talk with me. He told me what to expect and that there would be no contact for the first 60-90 days and that I would also not get updates from the staff. He said no news is good news. He told me that I needed to attend two onsite recovery meetings before our first visit and that I could see the NLB Counselor as needed. He encouraged me to go to meetings and take care of myself.

I walked out to tell Brad goodbye. At that moment, I wad D-O-N-E. We exchanged a light and awkward hug and I said to him, "I think we are done, but if you want to have a relationship with your children then you will stay here and get some help." He nodded and turned to walk down the hill to his new life, while I got into my car and drove away towards mine.

I really expected to be emotional and to cry all the way home but I didn't. The most overwhelming emotion I felt was relief. I was so thankful that Brad was in a program, that he was safe and hopefully in a position to get better. I was glad he was finally there because the days leading up to that NLB drop off had been quite tumultuous. The ten-months-plus journey had begun. My drive home was peaceful. I felt such resolve to go home and care for our kids in his absence; and the Lord really gave me a tenacity that I am so thankful for because it served me so well those first few months.

I went back home, loved on my kids, and went back to work. Another God detail of this story is that for ten years I had been in retail banking, so my office was always literally right in the middle of the bank lobby. As a result, I had to be chipper and customer service ready ALL day, everyday. Then in 2009 just as the banking and the economy were plummeting, God provided me a job in a completely different industry. It was a huge learning curve but I could work from home when needed, it was more of a back office operation, and I was the boss of the building so I could literally stay holed up in my office and hardly see anyone else. What a blessing that was during those first few months of 2013.

I continued going to counseling, continued to seek God and other wise mentors in my life but I still thought I was done, and I was ready to start googling divorce attorneys but God. God intervened and used an incredibly wise friend to speak to me. This friend's name was BT and we had worked together in the banking industry for years. He had recently gone through a divorce that he didn't ask for and he did not sugarcoat how awful it was. Because of all that, BT encouraged me to not give up yet. He said, "Listen, I know you are sick and tired of it all and it has been too much for too long but this is the one thing you have never tried (long term rehab) so what if this works? Wouldn't you hate to make a permanent decision based on temporary feelings?" He and some others said to me, "You don't have to do anything right this minute. Brad is gone for the rest of the year so why not just wait and see what happens?" I thought about all that and how sad I would be if I divorced him now and then he ended up getting clean and being the old Brad, the one that I fell in love with all those years ago.

I was a few days in and had not had time to grieve. I was running on sheer adrenaline because there was so much to do. However, soon after I got the chills and fell really sick. The kids got into everything around the house and it felt like my worst nightmare was coming to life. I had prayed that I would not get sick while Brad was away because there would be no one in the house to help me. I didn't expect it to happen so soon. I trudged through until morning, got the kids to school, went back to bed then to see my doctor. I was diagnosed with a bad sinus infection. Vicki brought me lunch and picked up the kids from school. Mom came when she got off work, fed the kids, handled baths and got them down for the night. It surely takes a village...

2/27 Journal Entry to Brad:

"Yesterday, Bella did not want to go to ballet, so I told Law to give her a pep talk. He walked into her room wearing his Upward basketball tee shirt and said "Bella, do you see all these stars?" Bella said, "Yes, let me count the green ones" and Law said, "Well, I got all of these because I worked hard and practiced so I would be a great basketball player. So, if you want to be a great ballerina then you have to practice too. All great ballerinas practice hard." Bella was not impressed so he looked at me and I whispered, "Tell her it is only until the end of the school year and it is only one hour long." He did that and she agreed to go. It was a proud Momma moment and something I would have immediately called to tell you if I could. That night, Bella told me not to be sad because you are in our hearts and we can talk to you. She said that you can't talk back but you are there. She told me we have pictures and your dresser is still in my room. She cried once she understood just how long we would be without you."

2/278 Journal Entry to Brad:

"I have wondered many things recently. Like are you a pathological liar? Are there things that happened that you have not yet admitted? Do you truly love me? A logical mind would say no but I wonder if the real you does or maybe you don't at all. Maybe I just give up because you don't love me at all. Unsure about it all – I will continue to ponder. I miss you at night. The cold winter nights when I crawl into bed and I don't have a warm body to snuggle up to. My little snuggle bug, BG is usually there but it is not like having you. I miss you and I love you. I pray for you all day, every day and I hope this will be your ticket to true recovery and long term sobriety.

Fun fact: Do you know how long a gallon of milk lasts in your absence? Like 2-3 weeks! I actually just had some expire. WTH?"

CHAPTER 13
March Madness

3/2 Journal Entry to Brad:

"I am on such a rollercoaster. I was sad because you were not there tonight to watch Law's baseball scrimmage. He started in right center and then played catcher every other inning. I don't know if it was a good thing or not, but he was so proud! He loved the catching equipment. He even caught some of the pitched balls. He only batted twice – the first time he struck out and he argued with the coach that he gets six pitches because that is how it was in practice. Hope you are well."

3/13/13 Journal Entry to Brad:

"The kids and I went to church today, came home, ate lunch, rested then went to the Museum. I didn't miss you much today. Getting out of the house on Sundays is actually easier without you. We get out on time and there is no drama or staying in the bed until the last minute. It is 9:30 p.m. now and I just let the kids get out of bed and come sit with me on the couch. *Gator Boys* is on TV and BG just said that if you were here we would pull out the couch bed and watch *Elf*. We are adjusting to your absence. It feels like you are dead. Dead to us at least."

3/17/13 Journal Entry to Brad:

"Tonight was hard for the kids. They seem to have some anxiety and feel insecure. Charles and Vicki picked them up from school and Charles took Law to baseball practice so I could work out. We had dinner at home with them and Law had a meltdown over BG finishing first and getting her dessert before him. He is also worried every time Charles and Vicki pick him up that they won't see me or that something is wrong. It is mostly Law because Bella is too young to put it all together. You have to understand all the hurt, anxiety, and insecurity you have caused our children. I hope you will finally get to the end of yourself and realize the gravity of the situation that you have caused and what we all now face. After Law's meltdown, I cradled him in my arms and he looked up at me and said, "I just want him back" and we both cried and talked. He is having a hard time understanding how long you will be gone. He asked about his birthday again and said he wants to visit you on his birthday so you wouldn't miss it. BG talked about you a lot too. She also cried because she wants her Daddy. So sad. Looking forward to a night with Lawson while BG goes to Mom's. I am questioning so many things today but trying to hold on to the promises of Jesus."

3/9/13 Journal Entry to Brad:

"Our son is getting baptized tomorrow. Sorry you are missing it. He is very excited and says it is the most important decision of his life. One of our dear friends asked if I thought I should hold off on the baptism until you got home. I said no, because Lawson has committed his life to Christ and we are going to celebrate that. Lawson is ready and we aren't going to wait for you to get your act together.

Earlier today on the way to baseball practice he said, "Mom, when Dad gets back I will be very happy and I am gonna hug him a lot and you know what else? If he ever feels sick with a stomachache or headache, I am going to read the labels before he takes anything. Mom, what he is he allergic to? Is it penicillin like me?" Broke my heart.

I hate this disease and the man you became while in it. I am trying to separate the man from the disease but it is hard because they have been the same for so long. My sweet children are forever affected by this and it is all out of my control. Last night, I took Law to Taki and to a movie then we got frozen yogurt. We let the couch bed out and watched Netflix – it was a good night. Tomorrow he is wearing a bow tie."

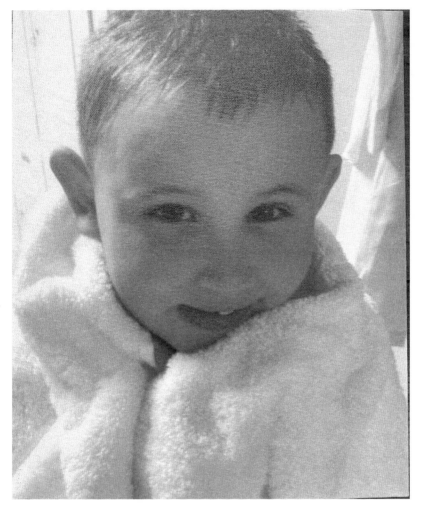

Lawson's Baptism

Something seemed to break every week. The first week it was the garbage disposal. Then it was Law's computer. Next up was the dishwasher. Ugh! I was going through the stages of grief. It was like a death minus the closure. I missed Brad. I missed having a husband. I wanted a husband but not Brad at that moment. I could not fathom living with him again, never knowing what he was up to. I didn't want to give up yet because I knew God can work miracles but the thought of living with an addict ever again is scary. I never wanted to live without Brad but now I am so, I don't know what direction to go but

I want to protect my kids and do what is in their best interest. I still loved Brad deeply but I didn't know if I could continue with him and I know that no judge will give him custody so he would be all on his own. How did this happen??? That question rolled in my mind over and over again each day.

God constantly used people, books, and even social media during this time to encourage me. I remember seeing this quote on Facebook and it quickly became a favorite: "God is too kind to be cruel. He is too wise to be mistaken. When you cannot trace His hand, you can always trust His heart." - Charles Spurgeon

Thankfully on the days Lawson had baseball he fell asleep like two minutes after crawling in bed. Bella was having a harder time falling asleep. Thankfully, during that stage I was resting like a champ, which was completely of because of God since usually I am scared to be in the house alone. I hear every creak and crack but suddenly I felt like I had this whole "living alone" thing down. It felt like a glimpse into the life of a widow or single woman, and possibly a glimpse into my future. There were constant reminders of Brad like when Bella turned on her tablet her little recorded voice said, "Hello everybody." Brad had programmed that for her. Once Bella said, "When Dad is not here, you can just pretend he is doing something for you or he is at the store. It's okay, we will just say he is out of town." She is so much like me, so matter of fact and an "is what it is" kind of girl. I guess I had probably taught her the keeping up and covering up part. "Keep up with all the people and cover up the bad stuff of life." Law on the other hand feels so deeply and his heart truly hurts. He wanted us to all to be together. I resented the hell out of Brad for bringing this insecurity onto our kids. They were so concerned that something was going to happen to me and they knew I was all they had so they were fearful of me going away too. I actually still loved Brad but I didn't know if he loved me.

It was mid-March and it was time for my first counseling session with the counselor at No Longer Bound. It was the strangest feeling being there on campus and knowing that Brad was somewhere nearby but I couldn't see him. The counselor (a female) was very welcoming and kind. She told me what a day at NLB looks like and she said Brad was on the maintenance team, which didn't surprise me one bit. It was a great session, and I felt really encouraged. I remember having a great time praying in my car on the way to the appointment, and on the way back home and just feeling really blessed. I realized no matter how hard it got, the kids were a gift and I just remember feeling good. My concern now was how Brad would fit into our lives after 10+ months away. I firmly believed that if God got a hold of him, there would be no limit to his potential. If this all worked out, I imagined Brad finishing school, working with other addicts, and having a HUGE impact on others for the Kingdom. (*Side note – you will want to make note of this prophecy.*)

Full disclosure – I didn't feel blessed every day and there were some days I lost it a little. Day in and day out was hard – it was hard to do all the things. I didn't even have energy to record it but it was just the little things that made me explode like the kids disobeying while I made a phone call or acting the fool in the grocery store. I remember one particular day that I just needed a few minutes to call ADT about an alarm problem and the kids acted like wild donkeys and in times like that it would become painfully real that I was alone.

My Mom would sometimes take one kid so that I could have one on one time with the other. That was super thoughtful of Mom and meant a lot to the kids to have that individual time with me. Every day that Law went to school post baptism he would say, "Mom, this is my first, or second or third day at school as a Christian." On day three I asked him if he had converted any souls yet and he smiled that little crooked smile that he got from his Daddy and said, "Not yet." He was a bible totin' Billy Graham.

I loved Brad and I missed parts of him. I longed to see the man who did not have the active disease of addiction because it had been so long that I didn't remember him.

3/17/13 Journal Entry

"Where to start? Today has been hard. I cried. Yesterday a guy came to put in a new dishwasher and thankfully he was still here when the kids and I loaded up to leave for a picture appointment because the car wouldn't crank.

He used his jumper cables to start my car and after the pictures, I stopped by Advanced Auto to buy a new alternator. The kids and I slept in the next day (it was a Saturday) and I think I just felt stranded and broken. The weight of my circumstances are weighing me down, and I just feel overwhelmed."

I remember feeling sort of paralyzed and just wanted to lay in my bed. I wanted to sleep but there was always so much to do. I would later learn that sleep is my body's defense mechanism.

Cherry Blossom time rolled around and it made me sad because our family always enjoyed all the festive activities. The Cherry Blossom Festival is an international festival that takes place in our city every March. The whole town turns pink for two weeks. There is always plenty going on, there are vendors, food trucks, carnival rides with fair food, animal shows, parades, etc. I remember feeling like I just wanted to be held. I felt like a baby. I longed to be loved and to feel love. I felt like the people around me were tiring and it was still so early in the journey. Sometimes, when I got upset, my family got upset too and it was hard. I remember crying and pleading with God as I prayed and as I journaled. The NLB Counselor had warned me that as Brad worked through the program and got honest, there may be some bombs dropped on me. The very thought of that gave me anxiety.

There was so much emotion during those days. I am a tough girl and I don't cry much but I was on a rollercoaster of emotions. It was like the rollercoaster of grief I had always heard about. First I was angry, then I was sad, and then a little lonely and then I felt weary and anxious. The list of emotions just went on and on. I cried quietly to myself then I cried louder in the shower and I felt all those feelings as they came. I felt such angst because I just didn't know what to do. I was leaning on the Lord and seeking his guidance, but I am also a very logical person and I needed to do the logical thing. I needed this to all make sense and the logical solution to this problem was to divorce Brad, take the kids, and move on with my life. But I never felt confident or at peace with that choice, so I waited.

I knew enough to know that when you don't know what to do you should do nothing at all. This doesn't literally mean do nothing at all but just not to make any major life decisions. So, I researched, I read, I went to meetings, I wanted to learn everything about addiction that I could. It was as if I was a doctorate student writing my dissertation on addiction. I read books, I talked to addicts, wives of addicts, divorced people, married people, I talked to my pastor, my counselor and other mentors/friends and I prayed A LOT. My kids ran wild, my family helped when they could, we did school, sports, and all the things as I wanted to keep their lives as normal as possible but it was not easy and it took effort. The raw emotions I felt during this time are reflected in my journal entries but if you could have heard my prayers, the emotion was there too. I let my kids see my emotion sometimes too. I wanted them to know it is okay to cry when you need to cry because the most important thing is to feel the emotions and not suppress them. I also wanted them to see how we would keep on living, and doing, because I viewed it as a life lesson in resiliency. Life is not always perfect or even good, but you always get to choose your response in any circumstance.

CHAPTER 14
Epiphany

Towards the end of March, my counselor asked me a relatively elementary question but not one I could get to on my own. He said, "Do you still love that man? If he can get straight, do you still love him and want a life with him?" The answer was unequivocally "Yes!" Of course, I loved him, I had loved him for most of my life and I still wanted to grow old with him, raise our kids, and keep our family together. Up until this point I was not certain that I was going to go visit when the call came. But then I decided that when that call came saying that Brad had earned visits, I would, in fact, go visit. I was curious if nothing else.

It felt like each time I had a moment of clarity or praise, I would soon have a setback. The kids were non-stop almost 24/7. There were many days that I didn't feel like I would make it. Times like that could make you understand how a mom loses it and drives her car into the lake. I was beginning to feel like people were over it - just like a death – others had moved on, and I was still there stuck in the mud and muck as time went on.

I am so thankful that I recorded memories of the kids during those chaotic times because if I had not written it down I would not remember the silver linings or the sweet gestures in the midst of the storm. One night, Lawson walked in and told me he knew it was tough to be a single parent so he was going to cut me some slack. I told him that I just needed him to stay in bed once I put him there. I told him what a blessing he is and then he showered me with words of affirmation. He went and kissed his sleeping sister on the head. He is a good man of the house.

Notes from a 2013 sermon I recorded from my church:

Pastor Tim explained how words don't mean much but actions do. It made me think of Brad because his words have been so empty and only time and his future actions would prove if he had changed.

3/19 Journal Entry:

"My beloved spoke and said to me Arise, my darling, my beautiful one, come with me. See! The winter is past; the rains are over and gone." Song of Songs 2:10-11 (I was ready for this)

Favorite verse from my devotion today:"

> *"Therefore, there is now no condemnation for those who are in Christ Jesus, because through Christ Jesus the law of the Spirit of life set me free from the law of sin and death."*
>
> *Romans 8:1-2*

"I still loved my husband, but I questioned whether I could be with him. "

3/20/13 Journal Entry to Brad:

"Today started off stinky and ended up pretty great. I feel so taken care of and I just realized this is the first time in a long time that I have felt this way. I felt held. I have felt taken care of by God all along this journey but today I also feel taken care of by the people in my life. Here is a snapshot of my day:

7:50 a.m. – went out to crank my car and it won't start. I called my assistant, she came over, we took the kids to school and then we went to the office. My assistant's husband jumped my car off and I drove it to the repair shop later that day. Before I picked up my car that evening, Mom called and said that your mom had called her to check in because she knew that the kids and I had been having some trouble around the house. Mom told her what happened today and that my car was in the shop and your mom said she wanted to pay for the repairs and for new tires so she called the repair shop and did that. That was such a gift! Mr. Bill at the repair shop fixed me right up and was so kind. He told me to call him if I had any more trouble or needed anything while you were away. God was in all of the details today. I also bumped into an old friend of yours who knew you were gone and he gave me his number in case the kids or I needed anything in your absence. God is showing up – He is holding me and that is all I need. I feel nourished. I feel spiritually whole and that is a good place to be. I pray that you will get there too.

3/22/13 Journal Entry to Brad:

"Law: "Mom, I think I know a way we can talk to Dad, (he has already tried calling your cell that you no longer have possession of) we can call the doctors and they will let us talk to him."

Bella: (in her stern voice) "Lawson, they will call us when he can have visitors." (soft hearted Law does not stand a chance with her.)

Law: "Well, I am not going through the summer without him so don't even start that. I wish we could live at the treatment facility then we could be with Dad and I could go to school and come home and he'd be there and he wouldn't have to leave or take us anywhere but he could be there and we'd live there too."

Heartbreaking stuff. Wish I could record audio for you. These are the days of our lives without you in it."

I was having a realization that I deserved so much more than Brad had been able to give. He had a mistress our entire marriage. Drugs is the worst kind of mistress because the consequences are so severe for everyone, but he chose it over me and the kids time and time again. It is foreign to think I could be with someone who just has me and that's enough. I can't imagine being with someone and not be constantly wondering what they have done, if they can drive, walk, etc. To feel safe and secure, and know that I can trust the other person, would be all new for me but I know it can be true for me and that I could have that one day. Probably not with Brad but I could have it. I felt like I could recover from the damage but I knew I could not endure more of the same so for those reasons I began thinking that Brad and I should not reconcile. I didn't know anything for sure but that was my gut during this phase of the journey. I was all over the place and knew I could feel different eventually or even tomorrow but right then I didn't think I could put myself back in a marital situation with Brad. I really didn't know if it would be divorce or a reunion at this point. I was told that I would know when I know so I am praying for great clarity and discernment. What if he did recover and get right in these ten months? Do I then give him another chance – another 3, 5, or 10 years of my life to see if it takes this time? I knew I couldn't endure this again and since there were no guarantees, I probably shouldn't even try. I never wanted a divorce, I guess nobody does, but I wondered if that may be my only path. Would that bring me peace? Everyone was telling me they would support me in whatever I decided to do. People will surely think I am nuts to stay, so I was still praying that I would clearly hear God's voice above all the others and that it would be loud. I am sure folks already think I am nuts and they don't even know the half of it. Does God expect me to subject myself to more lies and a marriage consumed by addiction and hurt? It made me sad to think about it all. I did sincerely hope that Brad was experiencing this Easter season like no other before.

3/24/13 Journal Entry to Brad:

"I just finished packing for the spring break trip to the beach. It is our first beach trip without you and it feels so strange because for the first time in years, I didn't pack a thing for you. I wish the bad parts of our history could be erased and we could be a normal family. We will miss you, I am sure. I realized today that I needed to buy a suitcase because you have ALL of our luggage with you! Thanks, Brad. I had to go in the attic today to look for a bag and Law said he liked being up there because it reminded him of you. On the way to church he said, "I'm not sure I can pay bills and work and do all the stuff grown-ups do but I trust in the Lord and I know he will give me strength." That sweet boy! I wish I knew how you are doing. We love you."

3/26/13 Journal Entry to Brad:

"Brad, we miss you. Yesterday was pretty rough. We left home at 10:15 headed to the beach. I got sick along the way (stomach bug) and it was awful. All I could think was what will I do if I can't drive us any further or if I pass out and it is just me and these little kids? It was such a scary, hopeless feeling. I had to keep stopping at random restrooms and locking the kids in the car while I went inside. By the grace of God, we finally made it to the Island. I rested for a while and then we walked on the beach and went to the grocery store. A strange man approached me at Winn-Dixie and it both scared me and made me sad. We all crawled in bed together at 9 p.m. and had a good conversation. Bella told me it would be more fun if you were here. I imagined having you to cuddle with on the windy beach while the kids played in the sand and I imagined you in bed with us right now. The kids say they miss you because you play with them and you love to see them having fun. Little Billy Graham held his bible all the way to the beach yesterday. He told me he weas worried about you and sad that you are gone. I told him he didn't have to worry because you are finally safe. With you gone (and all the chaos that goes along with you) for the first time in a long time I am just focusing on me and my stuff and on the kids. It is strange. This condo is nice, you would like it. Mom and Dad planned to join us for a few days but Daddy got sick on the way so they turned around and went back home. I think they would have enjoyed being here with us but we will still have a good time. I feel much better now and my stomach bug seems to be gone. I wonder how you are doing and if you can yet fathom all you have done and that you might really lose it all this time."

3/27/13 Journal Entry to Brad:

"We had so much fun today! It is still cool but gorgeous outside and we soaked up every minute of it. The kids and I shopped and had lunch near the Pier. We played on the playground, climbed trees, and walked on the beach. We went to the park with all the big oaks and Spanish moss. Tomorrow night, I am going to dinner with a local friend, she got a sitter for the kids and I am looking forward to a nice dinner with her. She told me today that she admires our relationship and how we have always prioritized couple time. She hopes we make it but understand if I can't do it anymore. It was so comforting to talk to someone who truly gets it."

CHAPTER 15
Scary Hope

3/30/13 Journal Entry to Brad:

"OMG. The Lord is speaking to me today. Bethany texted me a link to a blog and I read it. It contained a link for two free books written by an alcoholic who was also a husband and father. He got sober at the age of 35. It is like reading our life story. He was such a functional addict just like you. I cried over one of the verses he referenced "I will restore you the years that the swarming locust has eaten." Joel 2:25

Maybe there is still hope. That verse certainly gives me hope. This blog and book author says so many insightful things about life and about his wife. Here are some of the insights I took away from reading:

There are two different kinds of rewards. "When the Lord promises a reward, he first reveals the cost to be incurred and if we comply with that requirement, then we receive the reward. With Satan, he gives you the reward first and after you take it, then the cost is revealed and paid." *-Gary Morland from his book "From Beer to Eternity"*

Insights from Book 2 by Gary Morland *Scary Hope* and my thoughts:

"Encouragement to face the brutal reality that radical commitment is often required without any guarantee of results."

Am I willing to be radically committed to you? I do love guarantees but there is hope and yes, it is scary.

"Hope just means another world might be possible, not promised, not guaranteed. Hope calls for action; action is impossible without hope." Rebecca Solnit

Gary M. says that being a functional addict is so dangerous because nothing happens to make you quit. He said, "I hid my addiction and lied to my wife. That was not good for my marriage and even worse for my wife. What a horrible thing to do to your wife. But alcohol (in your case pills) as a god and I served that god." When asked of his marriage today Gary said, "I never knew anything this good existed."

I absolutely love that and hope I can say that one day too!

"Always trust what hope says. Discouragement is a liar; divide whatever it says by the biggest number you can find." Bobb Goff (*Sidenote- I had no idea who Bob Goff was in 2013 when I wrote down that quote. His books had not yet come out and he wasn't yet an inspirational superstar. As I write this book, I am actually taking a writing course taught by Bob. God in the details*)

"Brad, I have thought of you all night. We went to church and there were reminders of you everywhere. It made me sad to see all the couples. I thought of you as I sang "Our God Saves" and again when I saw the verse that says there is no condemnation for those in Christ Jesus. Pastor Tim talked about all the flawed people of the bible tonight and how God used them for BIG things. Peter was a murderer but delivered the first Easter message, Moses was a drunk, David had an affair, etc., etc., Jesus died for you Brad. I hope you get that this Easter. I asked Law to pray for you tonight and he said, "No, it makes me sad." Then he reminded me not to mention you. I prayed for you as I held Bella in my arms and held Law's hand. I heard Sara Evan's song "*Stronger*" on the radio yesterday and it really struck a chord with me. I know she wrote it after going through her divorce but it feels like my anthem right now.

Maybe, a little hope has been restored. I have run the gamut of emotions for sure. I am so tired and I need a break from single parent life but I know I am strong. I am a warrior."

As I wrote this book and I pulled out my old journals I came across pages of encouragement that Lord sent me during that season. He was always reminding me that I was never really alone. I want to share some of that encouragement with you:

"Most of the important things in the world have been accomplished by people who have kept on trying when there seems to be no hope at all." Dale Carnegie

"God uses broken things. It takes broken soil to produce a crop, broken clouds to give rain, broken bread to give strength." Vance Houner

"You're not always told the whole story up front. You may not know that until later. If you know the whole story, and it is long and tedious, you won't plan all the steps necessary to get there, you'll jump ahead. Sometimes the most important preparations for the ultimate destination are made in preparing for something else." Author unknown

"Aim at the result; that's the target, the thing God uses to focus us and keep us on track. But without a direct promise from God, hold the final destination loosely." Author unknown

"What if the depth of your wilderness was equal to the depth of the coming fulfillment of your hope?" Gary Morland

At this point, I wrote a special note to my husband and recorded it in my journal:

"Brad, I hope this is your defining event and you become a new man. You don't always have to be what you've been. The book I have been quoting a lot from Gary Morland is called "From Beer to Eternity" and he says it is the story of how he couldn't change but did. A nice guy's sad journey into hopelessness and the change God made. He says he drank three quarts of beer a day for 14 years but that was a long time ago. Now he is experiencing the ongoing, life changing reality of Jesus Christ. God, I hope that becomes your story for the sake of our kids."

4/1/13 Journal Entry to Brad:

"Happy freakin' Easter, Brad. I strongly dislike you at this moment. Law is acting like a fatherless kid and he has pushed the limits all day. He is now in his room at 8 p.m. where he will finish out the night. I am so tired of his smart mouth. He is just like you in that he always must have the last word. Today sucked. I am so tired and my allergies are awful. I would have given a limb for a nap today. Ma-Ma (my grandmother) told me that someone from the family said I looked so sad today. I wanted to say to that family member, "Well, damn, Einstein, I wonder why." My husband may as well be dead, I am a single mom who hasn't had a break in a while and I feel like I am drowning. I am not marking the days on my calendar until I can see you anymore because I am pissed. If I am honest, I am mad because I don't know how this story ends. Will we divorce? Will I find happiness? Will God save us AGAIN? I don't know but I know that I don't like you right now. Damn you. I feel like people are judging me and my kids.

Today, your Mom got all whimsical about the first visit likely coming up and I wanted to scream "Do you know what he has done?!? Drugs were only part of the problem!" I don't think she thinks I have any intention of leaving. Everyone else asks what I am going to do but your family says nothing because they would rather not know. If I leave then there is no barrier from the chaos. It would just be them and you.

The kids are in my face all the time. I am all they have, so I know they can't be blamed. Law actually asked me yesterday what would happen to him and Bella if I got sick and had to go away too? I assured him that I wasn't going anywhere, though I do feel like leaving for a long vacation some days.

As you can tell I am feeling very confused right now. I don't feel like I have clarity yet but maybe there is some love and hope left? Folks always said we were like peanut butter and jelly so we have to make it right?"

4/8/13 Journal Entry to Brad:

"I love you. Try as I might, I can't stop loving you and I can't imagine not being your wife as long as you are alive. I'm crazy and this might all change tomorrow.

Okay, its Monday and I still feel love. You are who I want if you can be right. (I think). I have always loved you like Jesus does but this time is different because I don't know how not to love you but I still don't know if I can be with you. I am not Jesus so I am leaving it all up to Him and praying I can hear his voice.

Again, the Lord was so gracious in sending encouragement my way. My next entry reflects that:

There is hope. "I will send down showers in season; there will be showers of blessing." Ezekiel 34:26

On my desk calendar: (this is the second time this quote has appeared before me this week)

"Nothing great was done without much enduring." Catherine of Siena

"My sisters, whenever you face trials of any kind, consider it nothing but joy...and let endurance have its full effect, so that you may be mature and complete, lacking in nothing." James 1:2-4 NRSV"

At this point the kids were growing weary. Often when family mentioned Brad, Lawson would say, "Don't remind me of him," kind of like saying don't remind me of what I have lost. He didn't say it in an angry way but in a sad way. The kids soaked up time with my Daddy and they loved getting to see their Uncle Chase too, so any male presence was a plus for them. I know Brad's heart must ache for them. I have to believe that ultimately he wants to be the one tucking them in at night. I know I prefer to always be the one caring for my kids, so I am assuming he doesn't want another man caring for his.

CHAPTER 16
The Revelation

4/15/13 Journal Entry to Brad:

"I am not walking away yet. I want you – the real you not the man you became but the man that I know you are. If I can have it my way, you will get clean, find lasting recovery and we will live happily ever after or at least together, right?

I literally ache for your touch and your hugs. I opened your top drawer and there is cologne stowed in there and it brought tears to my eyes as I got a whiff of it. I hope to see you soon. Saturday was the Luke Bryan/Jason Aldean concert in Athens and it was awesome! I missed you because we had obviously planned to go together.

Tonight, Law asked me when you would be home and I said hopefully by Christmas but it may be longer. He said, "Mom! You didn't have to tell me that." I told him that was the truth and around here, we speak truth and there is no dishonesty so he asked and I told him the truth. He said, "I know, Mom, but you could have said 'Lawson, I'm not sure and I don't want you to worry so we don't have to talk about it or I know it makes you upset so I'm not sure.'" That precious boy. I love how he constantly teaches me. He is such a bright spot in this dark journey and he constantly lifts my spirits. I love you.

God was in the details of 2013 in every single way. Babysitters, church family – He kept providing. I asked a young, female pastor from church to babysit one night but she had a conflict so I asked another friend for some babysitter contacts and she sent me two names. I checked my messages and the pastor had sent me those exact same names. One of those girls came to babysit and my pastor friend insisted on paying for it as a treat for me. I had a great therapy session that day and felt really loved. I love being shown once again how BIG our God is. I sure hoped He was big things for Brad too – showing up and showing out. One night, I was cleaning out a drawer and I found a note from Brad (not by mistake) that was from a flower delivery on our ten year anniversary. God is everywhere reminding me of His goodness and that He is working even when I can't see it.

In one of the books I read about marriage, the author wrote "we are still trudging along. We are back under one roof – we are showing up for each other and trusting that we are married for a solid reason, even if sometimes the reason hides for a spell. We are building a friendship. It is hard but good work."

I hope that is us one day."

Once I reached this point, I began praying a very specific prayer and it was that I would know in the first moments I laid my eyes on my husband that God was doing a work and calling me to stay. All my friends were praying that exact, specific prayer right alongside me.

4/16/13 *Journal Entry to Brad:*

"All in a morning with Law:

He talks non-stop and I tell him I need to get dressed so I need him to stop barging into my room. A few minutes later as I stand dressed in the bathroom he asks if he can come in now and I said yes. He stopped and said, "Whoa, beautiful, that's the only three words I got for you." I said "Law, you make my heart smile," and he said, "I know, I think I could make the devil smile – it would be challenging though." Then on the way to the car he said, "Mom, when I was 3, I worried that I would go to hell." I told him that is a lot for a three-year-old to worry about. Then he said, "I know but now I'm baptized and I know I am going to Heaven and I've been hearing what you have been saying – that I am a blessing." Yes, yes, you are Law."

Slowly, I began trusting, believing, and claiming that it would all be worth it. That our marriage would be worth it if we persevered. Brad in his way and I in mine. I still loved my husband and wanted a life with him.

A few days later, towards the end of April, I went to NLB for a recovery meeting. I met some of the guys in the program with Brad because some of them were in my meeting with their parents. I met one woman who had a spouse in the program, but her husband only had a week left so we were at opposite ends of the journey. I hoped the next time that I made the drive to the campus that I got to see Brad. When the meeting was over, I walked to my car and drove away. Knowing again that Brad was close by but absolutely unattainable, was once again a strange feeling. I was just trusting the system and trusting the folks in charge knew what they were doing by keeping us separated. There was a time when it wouldn't have been good if I saw Brad and I didn't even want to see him until a few weeks ago. But now I felt like the Lord was restoring what was lost and I felt so much love for him. I just wanted to see him, hug him, and be reunited. I still loved him dearly and guessed I always would.

Fun fact: In 2012 Brad accepted a role as an extra for the movie "42" which was the late Chadwick Boseman's breakout role. It was a movie about the career of Jackie Robinson and his struggle to become the first African-American in major league baseball. The movie had just come out in the spring of 2013 and it broke records the first weekend it was released. Our little Central Georgia town is known to be a hot spot for movie filming and it was so fun to watch the movie knowing it was filmed in our town and Brad was visible in a few scenes.

4/21/13 Journal Entry to Brad:

"Today, in your honor, I bought a Mountain Dew at Walgreens and drank it. I miss having you around – I don't miss the disease or the chaos but I miss you. I don't miss constantly looking over my shoulder to check for symptoms of drug abuse but I miss my husband. I miss sitting beside you at church. Funny story for you: You know how we can't let Lawson watch regular TV because of the commercials? He will call the numbers and try to get $100 back or whatever. The other night he ran to me and said, "Mom, there is an auction and you can turn in really old stuff for money. Wonder how much we could get for Ma-Ma?" (my grandmother and Law's 80-year-old great grandmother)

Then he saw an attorney commercial and asked me if I had taken something that started with "z" when I had him or Bella. I said no and he said, "Good, because you could be entitled to something."

4/22/13 Journal Entry to Brad:

"We are having journal time right now. Since I journal and find it so helpful, I thought the kids might too, so as I write, the kids are writing to you too. It is a sweet time of stillness that we get together. Still missing you here. Unsure of what you might be feeling. Do you love me? Do you want to continue building a life together? What bombs might you drop on me when I see you? If I am honest, I am worried that you may not really want to be with me since you have been high most of our marriage. I am soaking up these days minus the chaos and just loving the kids and taking care of myself. It really has been exhausting being married to you for these last eight years or so."

The kids' birthdays were about a month out at this point so I began planning their party. Much to their dismay, it would be a joint party this year because planning one party was all I had in me. It was strange to think about Brad not being there for it. I remember talking with him after his six weeks at Penfield and we talked about how he missed Law's first haircut. He said he missed that but wouldn't miss anything else but yet, here we are. Now he was going to miss holidays, birthdays, and the start of a new school year. God, I hoped this was going to be it. Our kids deserved better. I had made up my mind that I would never again live with an addict who is in active addiction and even though I knew I would be okay no matter what, our kids needed their Dad. I desperately prayed to God. "God, I hope you are changing him right now and working in his life. We want him back but only if he has a heart change and is healthy."

My ultimate desire was to have Brad back and our family together but it was also freeing and empowering to know that if that didn't happen, I could make that work too and I would be okay. I didn't "need" Brad anymore but I wanted him. I knew I could do this alone if it came to that and that felt so good. I did not plan any of this and found myself in a sink or swim situation but being that situation taught me so much and one of the greatest lesson was that I could do life without my man if I needed to. All of this took place about 65 days in.

4/26/13 Journal Entry to Brad:

"I'm so tired of doing this by myself. I mean I can do it but it still kinda stinks. One kid free night was not enough – I need at least two. It is 7:12 p.m. and I just want to lie down and sleep. Sometimes, I want to go out to dinner with someone and sometimes I just want to make out. Wish you could be here to help with those things. Oh well, you're not and won't be for a long time. Sad story isn't it?

Jarvis Jones from back home was a first round draft pick for the Steelers. The kids have not been writing in their journal lately. Law told me that I write enough for all of us."

As you know, I often recorded the things the kids said in Brad's absence and one day around this time Bella walked in from playing outside and said, "Momma, I hit my knees, put my hands together and prayed to Jesus and to God. I said "dear God, please help me be good to my Mom. Give me strength to help. Then I stood up, put up my hands and blew a kiss." Good job, BG. I know Jesus and God heard you.

I have mentioned how God routinely gave me doses of encouragement when I needed it most and one particular morning, I found myself getting ahead of things as I worried about the next seven or eight months and I felt overwhelmed.

About the time I was feeling those feelings, the counselor from NLB called. I got so excited at first because I thought it was "THE" call saying Brad had earned visits, but she was just checking in and did tell me that she thought visits would be starting soon. She spoke so highly of Brad. She told me that Brad's tender heart, the one that both his Mom and I had spoken about is still there. (In my head I thought – thank God he can still feel!) She said he was so verbal and tuned in and that he had been so open and forthcoming which was refreshing for her because she usually has to pull info out of the men she sees. She told me that she doesn't see any reason that Brad won't become the husband I need or the man God wants him to be. She also said that she told Brad that I was a very strong and purposeful woman and Brad said he knew that and that he owed me so much. I cried and thanked her for calling. She wanted me to look at my calendar to see when I can meet with her and Brad after he gets visits. I had all my prayer warriors praying the call would come soon.

It was the end of April and a little more encouragement came my way:

"See! The winter is past; the rains are over and gone. Flowers appear on the earth; the season of singing has come." Song of Songs 2:11-12

CHAPTER 17

April Showers bring
May flowers (I hope)

5/2/13 Journal Entry to Brad:

"Current events:

Bethany is pregnant – you will miss the birth because she is already 13 weeks.

There was a bombing at the Boston Marathon.

There is flooding in some parts of the country and massive snow in others. End of the world kind of stuff. In a nutshell, Jesus may come back before you get out."

(Sidenote: As I look back over my journals, there are some places where I would now tell that girl (me) to buck up and that it would be okay and that even though she doesn't understand or know what is happening, Jesus is writing this story and it is gonna be a good one. I would probably also warn her that a pandemic is coming in 2020 and she hasn't seen nothing yet!)

It was early May and I wasn't journaling as much as usual. I was mad again because I got a call from NLB earlier in the week and again, I just knew it was "THE" call saying I could come visit but really it was just the counselor telling me she was afraid she got my hopes up when we talked a week ago because it would probably still be a while before Brad's class earned visits. During those days of me not writing we survived a family birthday party and staph infection (Law). I was angry that it had been so long and knew I could no longer count on the 90 day mark for visits since the NLB class before Brad had gone over 100 days before receiving visits. The Lord was working on my heart because he knew I LOVED a plan and often found my security in having a plan for everything instead of in Him. It kind of felt like Brad was never coming back. It was so surreal. I never wanted to be a single mom but there I was. Not because of consequences from my choices but from my husband's. That is a hard pill to swallow. The days were long no matter how much help I had and ultimately, I knew the buck stopped with me. Law and Bella's birthday party was coming up and I was praying there would be a good crowd but knew there would still be a huge void. There wouldn't be a fun Dad in the pool playing with all the kids. Not my kid's dad anyway. I was praying I could get the good feeling back before the call came and I hoped NLB never called again unless it was "THE" call. I started reading through the journal I gave Brad on our wedding day. I think I just wanted to feel the nostalgia and how it used to be in happy times, before all the hurt. I was so naïve and starry eyed but I saw a side of Brad in that journal that I had long forgotten because that man had been gone for so many years.

5/8/13 Journal Entry to Brad:

"Yesterday stunk. It just needs some bullet points:

- Took the dog away so pest control could come and then they didn't show up.
- Why was pest control coming you ask? Because carpenter bees are literally drilling holes in the back door.
- Left work at 2 to pick Bella up and get her to the dance studio for pictures only to find out we were there on the wrong day.
- Law's baseball game left a lot to be desired."

5/9/13 Journal Entry to Brad:

"Today, I took Bella to the doctor and she has strep. Even though a lot happened over the last couple of days, God is still showing up and reminding me to find rest in Him.

Today is Mom and Dad's anniversary – 38 years! Recently I laid down with Bella and I had one of your shirts on that I sleep in and she said she wanted one. I got her a peach colored Polo shirt and that little miss slipped it on right over her night gown. It was precious.

I came across an article about Tim McGraw and Faith Hill today. Tim's main quote was that Faith saved his life in a lot of ways – from himself, more than anything. Then Faith said "Be patient. Put the effort in. Marriage takes work but it is a labor of love."

Will do, Faith."

5/14/13 Journal Entry to Brad:

"It is 12:06 a.m. and I am just crawling into bed. Everything is ready for Bella's birthday celebration in a few hours. Streamers and banners are hanging from her door, her birthday banner is in the den, chalkboard is on the stool, gifts on the dining room table and her special breakfast is ready to go. I am taking cupcakes to school, she has recital rehearsal and then we will go to dinner. I can't believe you are really not here for all of this. Hope you are well.

11:10 p.m. – Bella's birthday has come and gone. We had a great day. She got a pink 3DS device. I cussed you a little in my head this morning when I couldn't get the settings right but I eventually figured it out. MC, our next door neighbor is really rooting for you. She is so optimistic and keeps saying that you are working hard – I hope she is right. I need you to help me raise these kids. Nobody else on earth can handle the both of them like you and me. I can do it alone but it is not fun and is tiring. The kids hardly mention you anymore but I know they haven't forgotten you, I just think it is a grace gift. Just the fact that they are so well adjusted has certainly helped. We love you. Bella left her streamers on the door because she wanted you to see it and then she realized that probably wasn't possible so she said, "Daddy can still tell me happy birthday when he sees me."

By now it was day 86 and there was no word from NLB. I wanted to see Brad so badly at this point. It didn't seem like he was still alive and I felt like I needed to lay my eyes on him.

5/19/13 Journal Entry to Brad:

"Our baby girl danced beautifully yesterday at her recital! We got a special letter from you yesterday. I guess you are still alive because it was definitely your handwriting. It was exclusively to Bella for her birthday and I am guessing that was probably the rule. Today is day 88 and this just feels like cruel and unusual punishment. We had a busy weekend but I miss my husband and my helpmate. You sounded like your old self in the letter and I pray that you are becoming a new man.

A few things out of Law's mouth:

He drew a pic for you today on his computer – it was you and him under a rainbow and he said "See that? Those are God's eyes looking down on us and He is so happy." We saved the pic as "Law and DAD" and he said "I want his name in all caps because I love him so much."

I have been trying to get in the word because I know that God's word will sustain me and I sure hope this verse is going to be true of you:

"For though a righteous man falls seven times, he rises again." Proverbs 24:16

Please find healing at NLB."

May 25, 2013 Journal Entry to Brad:

"Bella just turned five and today, Law is 8. I have balloons, a doughnut cake and streamers for him. He wants to go to the Children's Museum, see a new movie, and to Chuck E Cheese for dinner. I don't remember if I told you about our new neighbors across the street. I met them last week and they need a HVAC man and I heard about you, but I awkwardly explained that you are out of town for a spell. It is a beautiful day today and I hope we can see you soon. I love you, we love you. Father's Day is coming up and that won't be easy for us but so thankful that we have my Daddy to celebrate."

10:22 p.m.

"Law's 8th birthday is officially over and we had a big time! Tonight, Bella and I snuggled up in our bed to watch "Lady and the Tramp" and I said "I hope we get to see Dad soon" and she said "I know. I wish we could have seen him today." I said I know, but we'll see him soon and then she said, "What if they call and we miss it?" I told her they have my cell phone number so we will get the call no matter where we are. She said, "And whatever we are doing, we'll stop and run out the door and drive there." Yes, BG, yes we will.

Current events:

- The Braves are having a good season
- There was a terrible tornado in Moore, Oklahoma. It hit two elementary schools and tons of homes. 41 dead and 20 or so were kids.
- Big scandal with the IRS – they tampered with taxes of the tea party members.
- A local mom beat her two year old to death.
- A Warner Robins woman was shoplifting at Belks and accidentally ran over her 4-year-old son.
- Men in the army are being charged because they had cameras/peepholes in the women's barracks.
- This world is going to Hell in a handbasket and I bet it is kinda nice to be secluded from it all. You never hear the bad news or any news for that matter."

It was the end of May and also Memorial Day weekend. Holidays were the most lonely. I remember buying a bracelet that said "Love never fails" but I often wondered if that was true because it sure felt like it had failed me. I had loved like Jesus did and I had shown love to Brad over and over and over but for what? God's love had certainly not failed me but Brad's love had. I didn't know how much longer I could go on. It had now been 100 days since I dropped my husband off and came back home. I could barely stand to go to church and pass all the "Christians" who knew where he was or at least that he was not with me and they said nothing. They probably didn't know what to say so they chose to say nothing at all and that was the most hurtful response. I wondered what Brad would be like when he got back. I can't imagine him being healthy for good. I was thinking about all of the things that he was going to miss: Father's Day, summer vacation, a friend's wedding, the birth of B's second baby, the start of the school year, Halloween, Ga/Florida game,

Thanksgiving, and possibly Christmas. I assumed since we missed the 60 and 90 day mark for visits, he would also not graduate in December as planned. That same day I came across this in an email and printed it out:

"*Everything about my life, everything that happens...*

The family I was born into

The circumstances I have experienced

My personality, DNA, wiring, and gifting

Is ENGINEERED or PERMITTED or GOVERNED by a SOVREIGN, JUST, LOVING God who always has three good things in mind:

1. *To develop my personal relationship and intimacy with Him.*
2. *To accomplish his purposes in the world.*
3. *To further his own awesome, immeasurable aims that are bigger than my ability to understand.*

THEREFORE, whether it is past, present, or future, I can have confidence and peace that somehow, someway, EVERYTHING FITS EVEN WHEN IT DOESN'T, & I will trust and cooperate with God in the fitting."

– Author unknown

That is good stuff! I strongly remember while I was walking this road that I just wanted to be acknowledged. I always preach to folks that if you know someone is going through a hard time, say something. Just acknowledge it. To ignore the problem or in my case, the family member who had suddenly gone missing, it felt like everyone was ignoring the hard conversations as well as ignoring the pain I felt. We always think the opposite of love is hate but really it is indifference. When you don't speak up then the person hurting feels indifferent. Don't worry about saying the wrong thing because as long as your heart is pure and your motives genuine then how your words are received is not going to be a problem. Give a hug, pat a back, send a note, tell them you are thinking of them, and the biggest way to show love (at least in the South) TAKE THEM A CASSEROLE. I just wanted someone to bring me a casserole during my hard year and I even thought about making Casserole the title of this book.

5/30/13 Journal Entry to Brad:

"I love you, I love you, I love you. Isn't this rollercoaster fun? I can't wait until the call comes but I have finally released it ALL to God and it feels so good. The kids are going to Mom and Dad's this weekend and I am going to Hilton Head for a friend's bachelorette weekend. Yesterday, Law was telling me jokes and said, "Who has two thumbs and attracts all the ladies?" "This guy" and both his thumbs point towards himself. He is definitely your kid. We love you and are pretty certain that you are getting well for us. XOXO"

CHAPTER 18

Sweet Summertime

6/2/13 Journal Entry

"I missed the hound out of Brad this weekend. I wanted a future with him. I wanted to be at the beach with him when our kids are grown and have our laps covered with grandbabies. I was looking forward to every season of life with him. Gosh, I hope the call comes this week. But God has taught me so much recently. I learned that He has to be enough for me. Not my husband, not my kids, not my bank account, not my income or Brad's, whatever happens God has to be enough in my life. No matter what I am committed that Jesus will be the Lord of my life and I would find joy and be content whatever my circumstance because I know that nothing can separate from the love of God. I sure do hope it is God's plan for me to have Brad though."

Side note to the reader: God was so faithful while Brad was away. He was faithful in every area but was oh so faithful in our finances. He provided for us in ways that could only have been straight from Him. Like an overpayment or two on an old credit card account when I least expected it, friends dropped of Kroger gift cards or pizza, the family company continued to send his paycheck each week even though Brad was not there contributing or working. I even had dear friends who paid for counseling sessions for me, so I didn't have to incur that expense. It was all so timely and appreciated and I was well aware that not everyone in my situation had those luxuries, so I counted my blessings. I knew exactly who was driving it all and He held my future.

We were 105 days in at this point and I was still in counseling. I had some great sessions and worked through stuff I didn't even know I needed to work through. My counselor helped me gain a whole new perspective. The adage I was left with was "everything is nothing until it is something." Basically don't make "nothings" into "somethings."

Romans 8:28 "and we know that in all things God works for the good of those who love Him, who have been called according to His purpose." So I decided I am going to love and honor the Lord and trust that He is in fact always working everything for my good no matter how my story ends or what I ultimately desire. God is teaching me once again but like never before that my total and utter reliance must be on Him. Not on my circumstances and certainly not on any human. I was trying to live joyfully even on the hard days. I was still in the black hole of no info from NLB and my counselor helped me to see how the process works and how the program was working on me too. I told him that I resented Brad because I still felt like Brad was controlling my life and he wasn't even here and I couldn't plan anything because I didn't know when the call would come. My counselor helped me to see that I was the one who wanted to see Brad and at this point it is all out of Brad's control so there is no reason to resent him. He said I should keep making my plans as if NLB was not even in the picture and then when the call does finally come, I get to decide if I want to keep my plans or if I want to go visit Brad. Wow! I can be in control of that decision. That was monumental for me and I was thankful for a new perspective and for the joy that was returning to my heart. I was praying that it would make a permanent home there.

6/6/13, Day 107 Journal Entry to Brad:

"It is my lucky day! The long awaited call came today! I am going to finally lay my eyes on you Saturday and I can hardly believe it! I am so excited and can hardly sleep. Please get well because I love you so much! My friends are all so excited for me and are coming over tomorrow to pray and celebrate! I had an incredible, sobering meeting with our Pastor today. It was not at all what I expected from our conservative Baptist Pastor but he looked me right in the eye with a tear in his and said that if you continued to behave the way you have in the past, then we will be unequally yoked and that is not what God intends for me. So, if I needed to walk away, I could, and I also could know that it was a biblically sound decision. He remembered me saying once that maybe I was just called to be the wife of an addict and he disputed that thought saying he didn't believe that because that would not be God's best for me. That was the first time I stopped and questioned that statement that I so often made. Pastor Tim spoke to me as if he was speaking to one of his own daughters. I love and respect him so much and I know you do too. See you soon!"

That evening, my friend Katherine (the pharmacist from the early chapters), who loves all things fashion just like me came over to help me decide what outfit I would wear for my first visit. Do you remember my specific prayer request that I and all my girls were praying? It was that I would know the minute I laid eyes on Brad that God was doing a work and calling me to stay.

After my outfit was planned out, some of my girlfriends came over. We held hands, we prayed, and we cried tears of joy as we anticipated that first visit. Vicki was in Chicago visiting her daughter, so we face timed her and the rest of us sat huddled together in my living room. We covered the Saturday visit in prayer and then went out for Mexican and a margarita because you know "balance". The kids were with grandparents for the weekend because I wanted to do this first visit alone. I needed to check things out before I brought the kids into it.

I went to bed that night feeling so excited! It was as if I was preparing for a first date. I had butterflies in my stomach, my outfit was hanging up ready to go and I was excited to hit the road the next day.

The entire drive to NLB (1.5 hours) was filled with such sweet anticipation. Visits started at 1 p.m. on Saturdays. I will never forget pulling up on the campus, I had been there several times at this point but I didn't know exactly where to go for visits so I just followed the drive around to what seemed to be the hub of the campus. I saw men everywhere. I parked and began walking towards the house where most everyone seemed to be. As I began walking, I spotted Brad sitting on top of a picnic table with some other men. He got up and began walking towards me with tears streaming down his face and when he reached me, we shared the sweetest embrace of our lives. I am here to testify that in that moment, God answered my prayer so big. I literally knew at that moment that God was doing a work in Brad and was calling me to stay in my marriage. It has been my experience that God typically does one better or as my favorite verses says, "immeasurably more" and this was no different. Not only did I know that God was calling me to stay but I also knew that God was calling us to something bigger. Something that was going to require both of us. I had no idea what that was at the time but I was all in.

Brad and I had the sweetest visit and the best conversation that day. Brad's eyes were clear for the first time in a long time and we had real, authentic conversation. It was beautiful and I left the NLB campus that day with a heart full of joy!

6/10/13 Journal Entry to Brad:

"We had our first visit Saturday and it was incredible! So thankful for that and then today I get to see you again because we have a session scheduled with the NLB counselor. They also called to say you requested an overnight visit and it was approved! Sex! We get to have it soon!

I love you and I can't wait to spend an entire night with you next week! (those were some glorious nights because we knew they weren't going to come around too often)

Soon more encouragement came my way:

Romans 8:18 "I consider that our present sufferings are not worth comparing with the glory that will be revealed in us."

"But hope that is seen is no hope at all. Who hopes for what he already has? But if we hope for what we do not yet have, we wait for it patiently." Romans 8:24-25

"And we know that in all things God works for the good of those who love him, who have been called according to his purpose." Romans 8:28

"If God is for us who can be against us? He gave us his son, how will he not also graciously give us all things?" Romans 8:31-32

Nothing can separate us from the love of God – what a promise! NLB's Facebook status was so good, it was a quote from Tim Keller that said "Jesus must become more beautiful than our idols."

6/14/13 Journal Entry to Brad:

"Today is the day that the kids got to see you for the first time. They were so excited! They giggled and talked the entire drive to NLB. When we arrived, it was similar to my first visit. We pulled down the driveway and there were lots of people around the picnic tables and basketball goal. We parked and got out and you came running but you didn't have to go far because Law and Bell were already running towards you. It was the most beautiful scene as you scooped them into your arms. I am forever thankful that I pulled out my phone and asked the three of you to turn around and I captured those sweet smiles. It is hands down my favorite picture of all time! We had a lovely day together and you got one on one time with the kids while I went to a family recovery meeting. They got to run and play and just soak up time with you. Lawson told me he climbed trees and Bella said she held your hand most of the day. Before we knew it, it was 7 p.m. and it was time to say goodbye because visiting hours were over. Six hours is a gracious amount of time to visit but not nearly long enough. The kids were too happy to be sad though and we talked and sang all the way home."

PERHAPS THE REASON HE WAS SEPARATED FROM YOU FOR A LITTLE WHILE WAS THAT YOU MIGHT HAVE HIM BACK FOREVER—
PHILEMON 1:15

The kids' first visit

For those first two weeks (my solo visit and the visit with the kids) you were allowed to visit on campus from 1 p.m. to 7 p.m. The third week we were allowed an overnight visit meaning we visited like normal on campus from 1-5 then we were allowed to leave and check into a local hotel (NLB chose the hotel and made reservations) where we spent the night. The next morning, we had breakfast downstairs at the hotel and then drove back to NLB (just a few miles away) and we followed the NLB vans to church. Those visits went on for a couple of months and then after Inner Healing (the next to last phase of the program) Brad began to get 24 hour visits which allowed him to come home and spend the night and he had to be back by 5 p.m. on Sunday.

6/19/13 Journal Entry to Brad:

"This morning Law said, "Give me a hug. I miss my Momma. I miss my Daddy and I miss my Momma and Daddy together. I want you to be happy. I'm sad cause I miss Dad but I am sad because you miss him the most. You've known him the longest, I have known him for 8 years and Bella has known him for 5 but you knew him all that time and then some." He is definitely your child – his tender heart is so precious. He hurts for himself and also for me."

We finally made it to the end of June! I missed Brad but I was absolutely ecstatic over the time I had with him each weekend. He had changed so much already and I couldn't imagine what the final product would be like. I was so excited for what could be – what he could be, what we could be, what our kids could be. There is no limit to what a sober Brad can do. I felt like I had a glimpse into what our future could be and it was exciting! I love this new man! I was always excited to go visit but it was always so hard to leave when the visits were over. I rejoiced and prayed all the way home after my last visit and told the Lord I wanted to bring Brad home but I knew he had to finish the program and there was still work to be done. Until the time came for him to be home for good, I decided to cling tight to the sweet memories we had made over the last several weeks. They were priceless. I thought about our intimate moments, holding his hand in church, hearing him sing praise songs, and seeing his tears. Gosh, I am so glad he is still alive.

We went on summer vacation with my family and it was such a fun trip but Brad was obviously missed.

7/22/13 Journal Entry to Brad:

"Today was not a good day. I have felt this impending sense of doom and like things were going to start falling apart again. I am tired. I can't focus at work and I have so much to do. I worry about so many things. I am feeling sort of like I did in the beginning as discouragement begins to creep its way back into my heart. To top it all off, I came home at 5 p.m. and the sitter told me that Law threw a baseball and it broke a window pane. It was one of the glass panes on our front door. When the sitter left, I melted into a puddle of tears by the broken glass pane. I need you here to fix these types of things. I called Daddy but he was at work and can't get here until tomorrow so we will have to sleep all night with a partially shattered glass pane on the front door. You know I am already imagining all the ways a burglar can get in. All of that made me sad, angry, and frustrated. But the precious kids came to my rescue. They loved on me and made me laugh. As I sat crying, I felt Law's little arms around my neck and he said, "Its okay Mom, it's just glass, its not like our family s broken or anything." I looked at him incredulously and said "But isn't it?!?!?!" and he immediately quipped, "NO! Me, you and Bella are together, and we get to see Dad on the weekends!" All is well in his world. Such a precious reminder to not sweat the small stuff. I did not get a call from NLB this week so I am assuming your overnight request was denied. The other wife in the program didn't get a call either so we are assuming everyone was denied. It is a hard but good reminder that this rollercoaster is not over yet. I hope God is speaking to you and busting you wide open! "The more difficult it is to reach your destination, the more you'll remember and appreciate your journey." Susan Gale"

7/29/13 Journal Entry

"I got the sweetest email from the NLB counselor today. The subject line just said "hello" and this was the body of the email:

"I just noticed your husband lugging some cords and things from a van and I could tell he had put in a good days work. I know that is a given – you know about his work ethic – guess I just want to remind you that the same way he takes whatever job he is doing very seriously – we can pray that he shoulders the full weight of being the protector and spokesman for his whole little family. I am praying for the day you call back to say "I didn't know he would step up like this.....this is what I have always wanted."

7/31/13 Journal Entry

"The call didn't come this week and that is the first time that has happened. I called today and was told Brad's overnight request was not approved. I asked about when Inner Healing (the next part of the program which would mean we couldn't see each other – visits would end and it would be zero contact again) would start but wasn't given an answer. I am still embracing the fact that I get to see Brad Saturday from 1-7 and hoping his Inner Healing class starts soon so we can get it over with. I had a great counseling session with KB today and he was so excited to hear about Brad's progress."

CHAPTER 19

Becoming

I t was now early August and scripture was still spurring me on. "Come back to the place of safety, all you prisoners who still have hope! I promise this very day that I will repay two blessings for each of your troubles." Zechariah 9:12

I heard on the radio today that during the storm in the bible when Jesus walked on water, he didn't stop the storm, He went to his disciples in the storm. That encouraged my heart.

8/7/13 Journal Entry to Brad:

"Wow. Yesterday I felt a lot of emotions. At 6:30 a.m. our house phone rang and it was one of the staff members from NLB calling to tell me that you had a minor accident and were sick. He said you had taken a fall and were headed to the ER. I never got the call from NLB about a visit this week so I emailed the front office and was told your Inner Healing class has started so your visit privileges have stopped. I didn't expect it to happen this way, we both expected to know that our last visit was our last visit and to have one more overnight but I have learned to expect the unexpected from NLB. I later found out more details about your accident. Apparently, you had a severe sinus infection and were dehydrated. You were up at 6 a.m. per the rules and you went to the dining room with the other men for breakfast as usual. You and your best bud, Ryan had an argument the day before so he wasn't by your side as usual. You and a few other guys were sitting on the back deck drinking coffee. You stood up to go refill your cup and then went down like a falling tree. You passed out but only for a few seconds. You came to and realized there was a gash in your head and blood was pouring down your face. One of the interns from NLB drove you to the local hospital where you got some antibiotics for the sinus infection and your forehead got stitched up.

I hope your head and face heals quickly from your fall and most importantly that your insides heal during this blackout period. I am thankful for the beginning of your new relationship with the Lord and the relationships you have made in the program – I know those two things will carry you through. I love you and I am lifting up so many prayers and can't wait to see you again.

"Funny story: I called to tell Daddy about your accident (he was on the golf course) and as I told him what happened he said, "Dear God, I am glad to hear it because when you first called and said NLB called you, I thought you were gonna tell me they had kicked him out and I was gonna have to kill him." I was thinking to myself that he wouldn't have to kill you because I would."

Note to the reader: please note the perfect and sweet timing of the Lord. He granted us visits with Brad just as the school year was ending so we had weekend visits all summer and then Inner Healing (no visit period) began in August just as the kids headed back to school and all their extracurricular activities. I was amazed by the Lord's care for the details, His love, and His sovereignty. Thank you, Jesus.

8/8/13 Journal Entry to Brad:

"Today's Jesus Calling was written just for us! Jesus has been so close since this Inner Healing period began and He has beautifully orchestrated this whole thing. I am now thankful for the 107 days of no contact in the beginning because it makes this second no contact period seem like a piece of cake!

From Jesus to me: (Sarah Young's Jesus Calling devotional)

"I speak to you from the deepest Heaven. You hear me in the depths of your being. Deep calls unto deep. You are blessed to hear me so directly. Never take this privilege for granted. The best response is a heart overflowing with gratitude. I am training you to cultivate a thankful mindset. This is like building your house on a firm rock, where life's storms cannot shake you. As you learn these lessons, you are to teach them to others. I will open up the way before you, one step at a time." Psalm 42:7; Matthew 7:24-25 (this was a prophecy that would later be fulfilled – keep reading)

More encouragement that was recorded in my journal:

"Your deepest life message will come out of your deepest pain." Rick Warren

"My God can buy back the worst season of my life and turn it around into such praise and testimony." Beth Moore

"And the God of all grace, who called you to his eternal glory in Christ, after you have suffered a little while, will himself restore you and make you strong, firm, and steadfast." I Peter 5:10

"I will restore to you the years the swarming locust has taken." Joel 2:25

"You don't have to wait for the storm to pass – go be awesome in the rain." Author Unknown

It was mid August and I knew that Brad must be putting in some good work and finding real healing because Satan was attacking like wildfire at our house. I knew we were in the midst of spiritual warfare. We had recently had so much to celebrate and because there was so much victory, Satan was counter attacking.

Case in point. The very next day after recording all of those words about the work Brad must be doing, I dropped the kids of at school and made my way to my office just like every other morning. But, this morning I "gently" hit a curb and busted not one but two tires. Two of my brand NEW tires! I pulled off on the next street past the curb and waited for the tow truck to come get my car.

I had a stye on my eye so I had to hitch a ride to the eye doctor to get some eye drops and patches. That same day I ordered Jentzen Franklin's book *The Spirit of Python* that is all about spiritual warfare and I listened to one of my favorite sermons that I had heard him preach one weekend while visiting Brad. Jentzen's church, Free Chapel, is where we worshipped every Sunday during our weekend visits along with all of the other NLB men. It was awesome.

My precious friend, AP texted me to say that she was under attack while her husband was in Inner Healing too and then she texted me a link to the exact sermon I had just listened to and she didn't even know about my whole day. She will be a friend for the rest of my life. We are war buddies and I love her deeply. I was praying that Brad would keep fighting!

"For our struggle is not against flesh and blood, but against the rulers, against the authorities, against the powers of this dark world and against the spiritual forces of evil in the heavenly realms." Ephesians 6:12

8/22/13 Journal Entry to Brad:

"Hey baby! I have so much to tell you and I wish I could see you, talk to you, and love on you! AP told me she saw you at church Wednesday night. She said she could tell that you wanted to tell her to tell me that you loved me. She said she has been around long enough to know the look – that wistful "I wish I could tell you to tell her" look but she couldn't talk to you because you were surrounded by men in the program and it was against the rules for her to talk to you. She said you looked good and were smiling. I have been sharing details of this journey and specific prayer requests with a private group on Facebook and their support and encouragement has been incredible. It is so healing for me and I think my testimony is going to reach people one day – a lot of people and yours is too."

We were nearing the end of August and I remember one particular Sunday that I had a strange experience at church. The night before the security alarm at home went off at 1:30 a.m. and it terrified me making for a long, sleepless night. We got up and went to worship the next morning and I literally felt sick in the car riding to church because I didn't want to go but I wanted the kids to go to their programming. It was so important to me to keep their lives as normal as possible through this unusual time. I felt something stirring inside of me and I think God has to be preparing me for something. I dropped the kids off and went to the bathroom. I stood in my stall and prayed for strength and that my focus would be on Jesus and not the people surrounding me. I was early and by the time I exited the bathroom, the first service of the morning was not over yet so I stood outside the worship center waiting for it to end. I literally stood there amongst those 2,000 people and wondered how I could feel so alone while being surrounded by so many people. It was like a scene from a movie where my character was paused, almost invisible as tons of people hurried and swirled around me. I walked in and sat down. I was contemplating going to the bathroom to listen to the message through the speakers. At that moment, I felt a tap on my shoulder, it was our dear friend, Brad T. leading the way for Kat and his mom, Barb to sit with me. Kat immediately knew something was wrong and as I told her what I just experienced with tears in my eyes, she said "Let me love you" and she hugged me, dried my tears, and held my hand while Barb passed the tissue. At the end of the service, I hugged Kat again and thanked her for loving me so well and she said, "Thanks for loving me and being my person." She is the Cristina Yang to my Meredith Grey.

8/27/13 Journal Entry to Brad:

"Law lost his first tooth today and BG has strep again. One more time and we will get her tonsils out. Law has been pretty difficult lately so hopefully we will make it in one piece until you get back. I wonder what you are going through right now. I asked AP to ask her husband how you are doing and he said you cry a lot which is a good sign and that you miss us terribly. AP's hubby only has 2-4 weeks left and then he is home for good! I feel lots of emotions during this time, I miss you, I resent you a little, I feel overwhelmed a lot. I think we have a solid soul connection and that my worst days here may be your worst days there. So, even though you can't read this in real time, I want to encourage you tonight. You may not be at the end of this journey yet but you are further than you were the day before. Focus on how far you have come, not how far you have to go. We have made it for 7 months already! 3 more months and we are golden!

Saw these words from Lysa TerKeurst today:

"If great things were not on the horizon, I don't think the enemy would be so bent on attacking us."

I know great things are waiting for us!"

We were ending the near of another month. It was the end of August and I felt so much love for Brad again. My strength was coming back and I felt like I was kicking Satan in the teeth! I knew that Brad must be kicking butt in Inner Healing too! I am still reading "Spirit of Python" and it is so good and applicable to life right now. My friend KM gave me a message to pass along to Brad today. She said she loves him and even has a soft spot for him but if he messes this up, she will beat his a$$. I told her that I thought she would have to get in line. I was praying the scriptures for my kids often and I particularly loved this one and it was my main prayer over Brad during those days:

"Heavenly Father, thank you for the special gift you have given Brad. Show him how his gift differs from the gifts you have given others and let him be generous, diligent, & cheerful using it." Romans 12:6-8

I believe God has big plans for Brad and I can't wait to see what is in store.

CHAPTER 20
August turned to September

9/2/13 Journal Entry to Brad:

"Hey, sorry that I have been absent for a while. I have been kind of mad again – old resentments resurfacing. It is so hard. Parenting without a male counterpart is hard and it is harder because I can't see you or talk to you at all. Lawson has been difficult lately, but we had a sweet time talking it over tonight. I asked him if he was sometimes acting out because of you and he said, "Yes, I just want him back and if he hadn't taken that medicine then none of this would be happening." His words were so true and he had no idea just how true but I was determined that he was going to learn that there are consequences to poor choices. He needs to be taught that lesson now while the stakes are still low. I don't want him to be learning hard lessons at age 35 when the stakes are so much higher and so many people could be hurt so we talked about that on terms he could understand.

Recently Law came to me and said, "Mom, I know it is hard on all of us with Dad being gone but he will come back in no time and we will be one big, happy family again. But if he gets up during the night because he feels sick then he has to wake one of us up before taking any medicine so we can check it." It broke my heart that my little fella was assuming that kind of responsibility. During one of the biggest spiritual attacks lately, the radio station *KLove* shared their encouraging word for the day and it was to always be joyful, never stop praying. So timely."

It was now early September and Brad was in week five of the Inner Healing class which means he only has one more class left! The kids and I kept busy and I recently had seen my counselor and he told me that I had graduated from therapy for now! It was a cool session and I was so excited – it was a victory so, of course, Satan counter-attacked. He used Law – the quickest way to wear me down. He had to stay at school daycare one day, right up until his football practice, which was a long day for him. I stayed to watch practice and it was AWFUL. He did not listen at all, he didn't obey or pay attention, and the coaches must have called his name 100 times. I was mortified and had no idea what to do. That was not my typical Lawson – this was a kid whose Dad wasn't around and it was clear that night that this kid had no male guidance right now. That is why my job as a Mom is so much harder these days because I don't know when to be really stern and when to cut slack and show some compassion because he is hurting too. Poor kid – it is just a lot to process. I know he will recover from this but it is heartbreaking to watch. I wanted to punch something, preferably my husband. I talked with the coach afterwards to be sure that he knew there was a lot more going on than just an unruly kid. He understood. We got home after that practice and I pushed the trash to the road and as I did, I hit a bump and the entire trash can fell over, dumping all of its contents into my driveway. It felt like the right kind of ending to my day. Sometime within the next day or two I talked to Jason at NLB's front desk, he was affectionately known as Fuller (his last name) around campus. Fuller made the calls to families to let them know when something was needed or that visits had been approved. I had grown so close to him because he was my only connection to Brad, kind of like a lifeline. I called him to let him know that I was going to the NLB furniture boutique to shop with a friend. I knew they needed to know so they could keep Brad contained somewhere else. Fuller was so sweet, as always, and thanked me for the heads up and told me he would be in touch as soon as Brad finished up his Inner Healing class. Made me think that would be soon. I hope so. I wanna hit my husband and I wanna kiss him. This is one wild ride.

9/8/13 Journal Entry to Brad:

"Hey baby, I wonder what you are doing. I wonder if you are thinking of me at the same time I am thinking of you. Church was better today – it was all about worship. I sat with VA, Vicki and Charles. I thought of you all throughout the sermon. It was so good, it was about David and how God chose him for greatness. David had victories and failures but point five on the outline really stood out to me. It said: "Those God plans to use to accomplish his larger purposes, He trains in (a) solitude (b) obscurity (made me think of NLB) and (c) through the monotony of rather insignificant, repetitive tasks (like the things you are doing at NLB) (d) through the reality of challenges that develop our character and competence over time.

"The conversion of a soul is the miracle of a moment, the manufacture of a saint is the task of a lifetime." Author Unknown"

It is now week 7 of the Inner Healing class. I am anxiously awaiting the call telling me that Brad has completed that class and we get visits back. I have decided that his particular class is not really on any sort of timeframe though, so I am not getting my hopes up too high.

My kids are so tiring but so precious. The things I have been teaching them are taking root and it is so beautiful to see. When I am down they encourage me by speaking the words that I have said to them back to me. "Mom, look how far we've come, we're going to make it," or "Dad will be home in no time. I love you."

9/29/13 Journal Entry to Brad:

"Good morning, love. I guess you are probably already at Free Chapel by now. I am sitting in my big red chair journaling, reading, praying, and enjoying the stillness of our home before anyone wakes up. It is a beautiful fall morning. I look forward to the day you are here to enjoy the seasons with me. I spent the day in Athens yesterday and savored a sweet 44/41 victory over LSU. It was absolutely therapeutic for me to be there. At the tailgate, everyone was interested in hearing about how you are doing. KB was the best. He already knew you were at NLB but at the end of the game when I hugged him, he said, "Tell Brad, we are thinking about him and we love him." Just another example of how much you are loved all the time, no matter what. Good Lord, I hope I get the call from Fuller at NLB this week! Hope to see you soon!"

The kids have a Jesus Calling book and sometimes I get it better than the adult version. "So when I tell you not to worry – I mean it! I know what problems you will face tomorrow. I've already seen them and I am preparing you to face them. So leave tomorrow's worries where they belong – in tomorrow. And when you do get to tomorrow, I'll already be there – without ever having left your side today." – Sarah Young, *Jesus Calling for Kids*

That particular passage is really speaking to me right now.

CHAPTER 21
Tricks & Treats

We slid into October and work was insane for me. One day, my cell rang and the caller ID showed NLB. Fuller was on the other end of the line and I just knew it was finally time! But it wasn't. He just needed me to send Brad more contacts. What a supreme let down. I was crushed but I remember that Fuller was so kind – he could sense the disappointment in my voice and said he knew it had been a long time since Inner Healing started and he apologized for getting my hopes up that this was "THE" call. He also told me that Brad is doing really well and has done everything that has been asked of him. He said that he just knew God has something in store for our family and he sees the beginnings of it day in and day out. I thanked him for that encouragement and he reminded me that the NLB counselor is available to me if I need to schedule an appointment.

I did just that and called the counselor, and I am forever glad I did because that talk blessed my socks off. She spoke so highly of Brad, just like she always had, and she told me there have been lots of new guys enter the program and when she asks them who they look up to or what older guy has what they want that they often say "Brad." I figured Brad must be floating like TP.

TP is a former graduate who the guys said floated around campus because he was so freed up, it was as if his feet didn't even touch the ground. I was so proud. I was reminded again that I have so much to be thankful for. I am so glad Brad is there doing the hard work. I can't wait to thank him for doing this for our family.

10/3/13 *Journal Entry to Brad:*

"Our baby boy made his first sack tonight! It was awesome! He has done great and you would be proud. Hope your week has gone well and I hope to see you next even if I have to sneak on campus.

10/9/13 *Journal Entry to Brad:*

OH my gosh!!!! Today was the day!!!!! Fuller called me around 11:45 this morning. It was awkward timing – I was in the car with my assistant and two of my employees, but I didn't care, I took the call anyway. I was over the moon! I said, "Is it time?" and he said, "Yes, it is time! He made it, you made it, you are done!" Fuller is the best and I am so thankful he was the person that kept me connected to you from week to week. Not only do I get to come visit, we get an overnight! I am floating on air and walking on sunshine over here. I cannot wait until Saturday! I can't believe this journey is almost over! We are on the downhill slide now and we have almost made it! I love you so much and I cannot wait to see you and hold you! I know it will be a sweet, sweet reunion and I am betting you will cry. A lot."

I, literally, stood in the kitchen last night and told God that I know that He expects us to pray for BIG things and then expect BIG results, so I said, "Lord, I really want an overnight," and today He delivered and provided abundantly! You will find out Saturday that you have a visit AND an overnight on the calendar! Also, my morning devotion started out this way so I thought the Lord was telling me that the call was coming! My devotion today from Sarah Young's *Jesus Calling*:

"You have been on a long, uphill journey, and your energy is almost spent. Though you have faltered at times, you have not let go of my hand. I am pleased with your desire to stay close to me." I feel God's love all around!

P.S. – remind me to tell you about the Georgia game it was another hobnail boot!

It was now mid-October and we had settled into the drill of having overnight visits almost each weekend so when mid-week rolled around and I had not yet heard from Fuller by lunch time, I called him. I guess we are getting the full NLB experience because he said there were some unmet expectations and visits had been revoked for everyone. WTH?!?!

I was so glad that Brad and I had spent the previous weekend together but I knew the kids would be disappointed that they couldn't go visit yet. I am clinging to the fact that this is almost over and that this situation is just temporary. The good thing for me is that I am going to NLB's annual banquet Thursday night, and will get to see Brad and share a table with him and some other guests for dinner and the program.

I ran across a good quote around that time that said "More marriages might survive if the partners realized that sometimes the better comes after the worse." Doug Larsen

Praying that is our experience.

10/12/13 Journal Entry to Brad:

"Last night I put the kids to bed at 8:30. Bella was asleep in no time, but I could hear reading and fidgeting. About 9:30 he came walking in the den with our favorite blanket wrapped around him. I was on the couch reading and he said, "Can I sit with you for a minute?" I said of course and he put his head in my lap and stretched out. He began crying softly and I said, "Baby, what's wrong?" he just said "I miss him." I scooped him up in a big hug and put that big ole' eight-year-old in my lap. I hugged him and told him that I know he misses his Daddy and I praised him for being so strong and brave. I reassured him that this was almost over and that we were going to make it. I am so proud of Lawson. He has been such a good big brother. I am so thankful for all that Jesus has done and is going to do. Your forgiveness letter was beautiful, and I appreciate all the work you put into it. I love you and I am so proud of you and excited for our future."

This is the end of my NLB journaling, but I want to share with you about the forgiveness letter I mentioned above. A vital part of the program Brad attended was writing forgiveness letters and not just handing them to the recipient but actually reading the letter to them. Brad wrote forgiveness letters to me, the kids, his mom, his late father, his brother, and my parents.

For the letter to his Dad, he took it to a nearby cemetery and along with his NLB brothers (just those in his class) he read the letter and buried it.

I will forever treasure my letter and I don't always know where all of his letters from that year are but that one I keep tucked in my dresser and I smile every time I see it because I am so thankful that we both did the hard work to make this marriage work.

CHAPTER 22

Ry Guy

I can't officially end our NLB journey without telling you about Ryan, and then I decided that he deserved his own chapter, so here it is. Ryan and Brad met at No Longer Bound and to this day, almost eight years post NLB, Ryan is still Brad's best friend. Again, we see God's sense of humor in this perfectly imperfect union. Brad had been at NLB for a few weeks when Ryan showed up. Ryan was a city kid from a fabulous beach town in South Florida and Brad was a country boy from Georgia. To the naked eye they couldn't have been more different. Ryan is 5'6, 170 pounds and Brad is 6'2, 220. One wears Mountain khakis and work boots, and the other wears Pelagic shirts and flip flops.

Ryan found himself in a recovery program just north of Atlanta, Georgia knowing that likely he wouldn't have much in common with those Georgia boys and would probably be the only kid from West Palm Beach there. Ryan was one class behind Brad and after Ryan's first assignment, Brad walked up to him and struck up a conversation and they instantly hit it off. I guess the rest is history as they say, or as my grandmother would say, "They were like Mutt and Jeff" from that day forward. When I met Ryan on one of my Saturday visits, I instantly loved him too. We soon realized that we shared the same birthday. God surely had Brad Sappe in mind when he created Ryan and me.

In 2013, these men not only became best friends, but they became brothers as they both fought for their lives and their families. Their common thread was addiction and in God's sovereignty it landed them in the same recovery program at the exact same time. What are the odds? They give credit to God for placing them there together because each is convinced they would not have made it through the program without the other. Ryan was one of our many grace gifts that year and in the words of Uncle Eddie, "It has been the gift that keeps on giving." Not only do we get to love Ryan but we have gotten to know and love his entire family over the years. We don't get to see them as often as we'd like (thanks to the 550 miles between us) but our love for them runs deep.

We got to be there in 2017 when Ryan married his beautiful Amanda and it felt like the height of God's faithfulness. Brad stood by his buddy's side as a groomsman and shared a sweet reading during the ceremony. Ryan's parents, along with his sister and her family are some of our favorites in the world and then we got a bonus as we also got to know and love Amanda's family through all of the wedding festivities.

I cannot forget to mention the star of the family, Ryan's precious daughter, Addi. She is the crown jewel of it all and we loved her before we even knew her. She was born in 2013 while Ryan and Brad were in their program at NLB. Brad had earned visits by then and Ryan had not so I might have done some detective work and found pics of Ryan's new baby girl on social media. I also might have printed them and snuck them to the boys at NLB. I promise that was the only rule I broke but Ryan just had to see that beautiful baby girl who looked just like him. Over the last year, Amanda gave birth to their precious Emmy, so now Addi shares the spotlight with her sister and they are a sweet family of four. God is so good! I really don't have words adequate enough to describe the relationship that Brad and Ry share. It is one of those things that you just have to experience. Brad, our kids, and I love Ryan dearly and the entire relationship is a beautiful thing. If you ever see them together, you will note they are both very handsome, they will both make you laugh with their almost identical sense of humor, and you can only tell them apart because one will be wearing shorts and slip-on shoes and the other will be in jeans and boots.

Just the other day, Brad and Ryan were saying that statistically speaking, after struggling for so long, neither of them should even be alive much less thriving the way they are today. They are an unlikely pair who found themselves in the same situation and in the same boat searching for hope at a program in North Georgia. They found each other and more importantly, they found Jesus. They also found the tools to navigate this life well and I will be forever thankful. If you have followed me long or heard me speak at an event, then you know I love to talk about how we serve a God of details, and we can often find Him in the details of our lives. I can see God's hand so clearly in the friendship of Ryan and Brad.

I can't end this chapter about Ryan without telling you a story that we still laugh about today. You remember reading about Brad's accident on the deck at NLB, the one where he passed out and had to get stitches?

I eventually got to hear the full story from some of the other NLB guys who were there that fateful morning and this is the story through their eyes:

Brad woke up that morning feeling sick and as he and some NLB brothers sat on the back deck drinking coffee, Brad told them he felt like he was going to pass out. He had felt bad for a few days, but he didn't know if it was just because he missed his family so bad or if he was really sick. Brad stood up to get more coffee and down he went – passed out. Ryan and Brad had argued the day before, so Ryan was mad and not speaking to Brad.

Ryan heard the loud thud of the fall, stepped into the dining room and while looking through the sliding glass doors he realized it was Brad, and he leapt into action.

Rumor has it that Ryan jumped over three tables and scooped up Brad's head and cradled it in his arms as he wiped the blood from Brad's eyes. Brad woke up and Ryan said, "Do you know where you are?" to which Brad replied "Yes, unfortunately I am still in rehab."

Ryan stayed by his side, cradling his head and assuring Brad that he was going to be okay and that the cut wasn't as bad as it felt even though blood was streaming down Brad's face. Once Brad felt like he could get up, Ryan helped him to the car that would drive him to the hospital. Brad and Ryan were reconciled at that point and can't even remember the squabble from the day before.

Thank you Lord, for the gift of friendship and especially for the gift of Brad and Ryan. We are not worthy of your lavish love but thanks for giving it anyway.

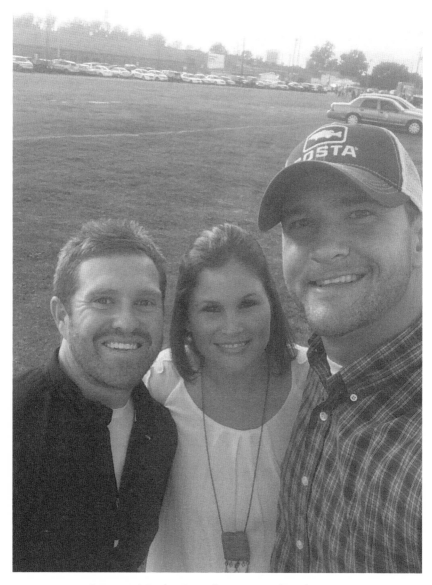

Ryan, me, & Brad on Ryan's first visit to our home in 2015

CHAPTER 23
The Rest of the Story

You have just read through our most challenging year to date and what we refer to as our NLB Journey. Now, let me give you the rest of the story.

I want to start by telling you one of the most pivotal moments of my NLB journey and that was realizing that I had to get to the place of knowing that I was going to be okay no matter what. I finally got okay because I knew I could truly be okay no matter the outcome. I certainly hoped like hell that God was going to restore my marriage and give me my husband back but I could not walk in freedom until I could say but even if He doesn't restore this, or even if Brad doesn't change, I will be okay. The really cool part is that God was telling Brad the exact same thing on his side of the journey. When Brad came home, we compared journals and it was absolutely amazing to realize that God was telling each of us the same thing and teaching us the same lesson. We were in the same storm but on very different sides of it. For Brad, God spoke to him one day while he was journaling at NLB. Brad was lamenting to the Lord about possibly losing his family and he clearly heard God say, "What if she leaves? What if she takes the kids? What are you going to do? Go back to your old ways of using and numbing the pain? You have to surrender and let me be enough in your life." It was in that moment that Brad knew that was the only way, so he surrendered and got okay with however the story ended.

For me, I was at home with the kids - suddenly a single, working Mom and life was not going as I planned and God looked down on me and said, "What about you? What are you going to do? Are you going to be angry and resentful about the way things are going or are you going to trust me, surrender, and let me be enough in your life?" Because of the work of the holy spirit in my life, I had the strength to just surrender and let Him be enough.

I want to encourage you that he can be enough in your life too. It is hard to imagine that when your earthly circumstances are not playing out like you had hoped, but if your sit with Him long enough, you will begin to trust and then when He shows you His faithfulness, that gives you the ability to keep trusting for bigger and better things.

CHAPTER 24

Lawson and Bella (affectionately known as Law and BG)

Many of you may be wondering how Lawson and Bella felt all throughout this journey. They have been gracious enough to share their thoughts with me. They were 7 and 4 in 2013 and are now 15 and 12.

Lawson – "I couldn't really process it back then. I knew that something was wrong and that Mom missed Dad and I missed Dad. Eventually, it weighed heavily on me and I realized how long he was going to be gone and that I needed to be the man of the house. Mom was pretty capable though so the responsibilities didn't come up too often for me but I tried my best. I loved going to the NLB campus for visits and I felt great joy when I got to see Dad and hug him.

I was really sad when Dad missed my baptism and my 8th birthday party, but I really don't remember a lot of details. When he came home in December, I was so happy to know that he was home for good. I have never worried about him getting sick again because it was so evident that he was a changed man and would never make those choices again."

Bella – "I remember coming home from school and Ga Ga and Pop were sitting on the couch and I could tell Mom had been crying. Then I just remember Mom, Lawson, and me laying across Mom and Dad's bed together in silence. Mom must have told us what was going on but I don't remember that part. Once we got visits and were able to go see him it was great and then we got overnight visits and got to spend the night at that hotel with the indoor pool. I remember the first time that Law and I got to visit Dad, it had been four months since we had seen him and we just ran and jumped in his arms! Mom got a special picture of that moment that we all love. I remember the fall season of that year and how the playground at NLB was filled with leaves and Lawson and I jumped in them all day. I also have memories of worship at Free Chapel and how we had to leave in our own car after the service and Dad had to leave with the NLB men in the van.

I distinctly remember the day that Dad came home for good. Mom went to pick him up and when Mom and Dad walked in, we were hiding behind the French doors in the dining room and we jumped out with party blowers and confetti to welcome him home. There was also a big "Welcome Home" poster on the wall. Gan, Gannie Faye, Ga Ga, Pop, Ma-Ma, and Aunt Meg were all there with us waiting on Dad and we were all so excited that he was going to be home for good!"

This made my heart smile because it shows the resiliency of kids and how they literally only remember the best things from that unusual year. To God be the glory!

CHAPTER 25
Christmas Blessings

On December 21, 2013, Brad came home to us for good. He completed the NLB recovery program and came home just three days before Christmas. I can hardly put into words how sweet that Christmas was. That year, none of us cared about lists or what was under the tree because we were just so happy to be together. All that mattered to us was being together and we vowed that as life got back to normal that we would remember all the days we had spent apart and how much we had taken for granted. I remember what a treat it was to snuggle up to my husband in bed at night or on the couch as we watched a movie because for ten months that had not happened so now it felt like such a luxury.

Brad did not immediately go back to work as he used those first few months to acclimate back to our home life and to pour into the kids and me. He made lunches and drove them to and from school and it was such a blessing.

Sometime in late January or early February of 2014, I went home for lunch and Brad was journaling at the dining room table. I heated my lunch and sat with him and he said, "I think God is calling me to start a program like No Longer Bound here. There is nothing like it around here and I want to help guys find what I found." He looked right at me and said, "Are you all in?" and I didn't blink before exclaiming "Of course!" It was a no brainer for me because just as Brad had so much for addicts who were struggling, I had such a heart for families of addicts. In March, Brad went to work for a local HVAC company (that is his trade skill) and applied to the local University to complete his undergraduate degree. I was working my full time job as COO of a local company, earning enough money for us to be comfortable and I carried the insurance for our family of four. Life was good and we were excited and hopeful for what the future held, certainly it would be bright!

CHAPTER 26

Disappointment & Blessing
(they often exist together)

On May 20, 2015, I was called into an unexpected meeting with the CEO of the company I had worked for over the last six years and in that meeting, I lost my job. I was called in and told very matter of factly that the company had been sold and most everyone was being terminated. I was one of them. He said the new company has their own COO and I was no longer needed. I was so stunned and shocked that I couldn't find my words. I just said okay, and walked out. I was instructed to go get my purse and then leave as quietly as possible as not to alarm any of the employees that I had so lovingly cared for over the last six years. I had never lost a job in my life and in this case I was the CEO's right hand so I couldn't believe he had not warned me and that he chose to let it go down this way. I remember having plans that night for a UGA alumni and season ticket holder annual gathering. My family of four was attending as well as my parents. I didn't want to cancel because it only came around once a year and we always looked forward to going. It was there at that event during dinner that I told my parents I had lost my job. I was afraid, tearful, and ashamed. The very next morning my journal once again recorded what Jesus told me through Sarah Young's *Jesus Calling Devotion*:

"I, the creator of the universe, am with you and for you. What more could you need? It is not so much adverse events that make you anxious as it is your thoughts about those events. Your mind engages in efforts to take control of a situation, to bring about the result you desire. Your thoughts close in on the problem like ravenous wolves. Determined to make things go your way, you forget that I am in charge of your life. Stop all your striving and watch to see what I will do. I am Lord!"

What a timely word for me!

In my journal over the next few days, I asked the Lord to help me see what He had for me in this trial. I prayed for confidence, the ability to hold my head up high, love my family, and to be a good example through this hard thing. I told Him that I trusted Him to direct me and lead me to the right place and the right job. I was reminded of one of my favorite bible stories of Moses leading the Israelites through the Red Sea. I felt God saying to me, "Don't be afraid. Just stand still and watch the Lord rescue you today. The Lord himself will fight for you. Just stay calm." Exodus 14:13-14. I was counting on it.

The story of the Red sea miracle has always brought me so much strength and encouragement because the exact same God who parted the Red Sea and saved the Israelites is the same God I serve today. His power has not diminished. I am human though and I ebbed and I flowed. Some days I felt held in His arms, I was confident and secure, and then some days I was discouraged and afraid. On those days, I prayed harder. I kept asking God to renew my mind and a few days later on May 29th, my *Jesus Calling Devotion* said, "I know precisely what you need to draw nearer to me. Go through each day looking for what I have prepared for you. Accept every event as my hand tailored provision for your needs. When you view your life this way, the most reasonable response is to be thankful. Do not reject any of my gifts; find me in every situation."

CHAPTER 27

Won't He do it?

I love the phrase "Won't he do it?" Some of my favorite podcasters use that phrase all the time and they even had a tee shirt made that says it. Of course I purchased it! They use it for real miracles as well as when they find a good pair of shoes half off, or their favorite football team wins a game and I love it.

May had ended and now it was June and my unemployed self would soon be 36-years-old. I prayed through Isaiah a lot, reminding myself that God would help me and uphold me with his righteous right hand. I was praying a lot about what to do, do I take another job, start a new career? Go back to banking or do I use this time to start our ministry? My whole journal during this time was mostly me writing out my *Jesus Calling Devotions* or recording scripture. I was searching and didn't have any real answers yet. What we did have though, was a vacation that had been planned long before I was laid off, the condo was already paid for, so we went. Logically speaking, it seemed crazy for an unemployed person to go on vacation but we just needed a happy place and something to look forward to so with our American Express card in hand, we took off! To this day it is one of our favorite and most memorable vacations! We loved it so much and had such a good time. You should always have something to look forward to, especially during hard times. Look for the joy and celebrate whatever and whenever you can!

By the end of July, the Lord had heard my prayers and answered. Bethany sent me a job description for a position with a local non-profit. On July 8th, I applied, had an interview on July 13th, and was offered the job on July 20th! I was going to be the Center Director for a local non-profit ministry. Not only did God provide me with a job working in a non-profit as I had prayed but it was considered full time with benefits and I only had to work four days a week! I had every Friday off! Won't He do it? He is still doing immeasurably more in our lives. I stood in awe of the Lord's handiwork and all He had done. I was amazed, fulfilled, and thankful.

Late in 2014 we found out that Brad's story was going to be featured at the 2015 NLB fundraising banquet so the film crew from NLB Media worked with us for months. The Banquet was set for October and I guess we wrapped up filming in late August or early September. Spiritual warfare was once again intense as we neared the banquet date where our video would be debuted to hundreds of people and then put online for the whole wide world to see. We were on the brink of the banquet and the start up of our own ministry. I don't remember the specifics of the warfare but I know it was there because I journaled about it and it was one of the many times along the journey that God reminded me that the weapons we fight with are not the weapons of this world – they are spiritual.

The day of the banquet finally arrived, and we were filled with antic-ipation. We had not seen so much as a snippet of the video we had filmed for months. It is a really cool God story of how we were even chosen to be the featured story that year. Remember that Brad came home at the end of 2013? I forgot to mention God's play on dates but if you remember from the beginning of the book, we got engaged on December 21st, Brad went away to treatment almost 11 years later on February 21st and then he came back home to us for good on December 21st. Anyway, in 2014, Lawson was in the third grade at a local Christian school. Every Wednesday was Chapel and different grades would take turns hosting the program. When it was third grade's turn, the music teacher asked if anyone would like to give their testimony and of course, Law volunteered. That boy has been raising his hand for whatever anyone asked for as long as he has been walking. Volunteers needed? His hand went up. A question to answer? His hand goes up. Give your testimony to a room full of people? His hand went up.

The music teacher soon emailed to say that all students giving a tes-timony on stage needed to have their speech typed up just in case they got nervous on stage and froze. I will never forget the night we called Law into our den and told him we needed him to write down what he planned to say.

He said, "Oh, no, Mom it's fine. I have it all in my head." I said okay, that's great but we really need to know what you are going to say," so he agreed to practice in front of us and I am here to tell you that Brad and I were reduced to a puddle of tears as we sat on our couch listening to our brave boy speak straight from his heart.

Chapel day rolled around and the room was full. After hearing a few other kids go ahead of him, I was so nervous – I remember looking at Brad and saying, "I think we did this wrong." All the other kids were great but it was rehearsed and was just them reciting bible stories or scriptures, not a real life experience and certainly not one that included someone going to drug rehab. Then it was Lawson's turn. As he began to speak all my fears melted away because I knew it was just what God expected from him and He was surely smiling down on all of us that day. Law stood on that stage and spoke straight from his heart. He talked about the year before and how it was hard for our family and especially hard for his Mom because his Dad was away, and she had to raise him and his sister by herself but that God never left us. He said his Dad is back and now he doesn't just tell him and his sister about Jesus but he tells everybody and he plans to start a ministry. It was the most transparent, heart wrenching experience straight out of the mouth of a third grader. There was not a dry eye in the room. Somewhere in the speech Law talked about No Longer Bound and how much he enjoyed visiting on weekends, and I thought that was incredibly profound and would be such an encouragement to the NLB staff. So, I emailed the video to the director and they immediately emailed back and said they wanted to interview Lawson for a social media video and would be in touch. As they talked through it, they realized that Law was incredible but the family story as a whole was super powerful too, and would be the perfect story to showcase at their annual benefit. We were so honored and amazed by how God was working.

The day of the banquet arrived and we set out towards Atlanta. It was a beautiful evening and we were surrounded by our closest friends and family as well as our NLB family. The video was a big hit and we were so humbled and honored to get to share our God story. God reminded me that night that our story was His story and we just get to be the characters and carry out the good works that he prepared in advance for us to do. In our God story, His power, love, and redemption are on full display. It has been quite the journey and I am so thankful for it.

I want to give a proper nod to No Longer Bound here. Our family is so incredibly grateful for that place and it means so much to us. For many years after Brad came home, our kids would thank God in their nightly prayers for NLB and we have always considered that property to be sacred ground. It was the vessel God used to save our family and we are forever indebted. So many chains are broken and lives restored on that piece of property in Cumming, Georgia. May everyone walk close enough and long enough to see the transformation.

The Destin vacation

CHAPTER 28
Off to the Races!

As we forged forward with the beginning of our ministry, we felt so small and insignificant. Starting a ministry is a huge undertaking and so from the beginning we prayed that God would do something so big that it was destined to fail without Him in the center of it.

In the next few days, after feeling the fear associated with doing something new and starting this big thing with no guarantees I heard a timely message from Pastor Jentzen Franklin. If you still don't know who he is, Google him and then listen to as many sermons as you can. He is phenomenal and his sermons and books have been life changing for me. You may remember that NLB worshipped at his church, Free Chapel when I was visiting Brad and I loved it. I missed not being able to attend the church once Brad came home so we listened online as often as we could. This timely sermon was called 'Dreams - The value of a dream.' Jentzen talked about how when we dream a dream, we become more like God than ever before. He said when God gives you a dream, critics and skeptics cannot stop it. Even if for a season you lose heart, the dream keeps working. He talked about the great dreamer of the bible, Joseph. He said when God plants a dream, there is always risk and danger in going after it. He told the story of Joseph and all Joseph endured at the hands of his brothers and then in Egypt. Pastor Jentzen reminded us that if God plants the dream in your heart, He will be faithful to fulfill it. He broke it down into every day terms which is one of the reasons people love to listen to him speak. Pastor Jentzen said, "We say I wish I could get a new job, but God says be happy were you are, be fruitful in the land of affliction. Grow where you are right now. Be faithful and fruitful, and soon it will become apparent you don't belong there anymore, and God will open up the next door." What a powerful word and I felt like it was just the encouragement my heart needed!

Do you remember me mentioning in a previous chapter about the trusted Christian counselor who told me to divorce my husband? Some time during the year of 2014, she reached out, apologized, and we were reconciled. I was no longer upset with her because I realized from the outside looking in, divorce was a logical and even biblical option. I think she cared for me so much that she just wanted God's best for me. I am so thankful for her wise counsel over the years and to still know her today.

I want to share one last journal entry with you about how we received our first resident well before we were "ready" to accept anyone.

December 15, 2015

"Last week we sort of obtained our first Cross Roads resident. It was a man that Brad knew from NLB, that we will call M. He came to Macon to work and live in transitional housing while he got his feet back on the ground and he wanted to be close to Brad so he just showed up. Brad went to visit him at the transition house and said the living conditions were awful and he just couldn't leave him there. He called me to say he was bringing M into the program. Excuse me? What program? Like we have a tax id number and we are an official non-profit but we are not a "program" yet. As I sat in my office at work getting all hot and bothered about what we were supposed to do with this guy just one week before Christmas, I clearly heard the Lord say to me "If you can't take care of one, how can you take care of forty?" The Lord hit me right over the head and I was so thankful. The Lord knows He has to speak real slow and clear to me. "

So, caring for first resident meant using funds from our first ministry fundraiser (a couple of months prior) to put him up at an extended stay hotel. Brad helped him find work and met with him daily.

That hotel worked for a few weeks and got us through the Holidays and then we got him into a one bedroom apartment about a block from our house and then to a three bedroom house where we took on three more residents and then a multi-bedroom house that would hold ten residents. God has not stopped surprising us since sending that first resident in 2015. His ways are higher than ours and I am so grateful. If my life had turned out the way I thought it should or the way I planned it, I would have missed out on so many blessings – at least a hundred or so that have come through our ministry.

CHAPTER 29
Leaps of Faith

Starting the ministry was a huge leap of faith but the Lord has been so faithful and has provided in every way every single day. There were many times after I lost my corporate job that things were tight financially. If you really want to know how much you trust the Lord, try trusting him completely in your finances. Most of us don't get there unless we lose something and for me losing a big chunk of my salary as I went to work for a non-profit, the loss was felt. I know I was able to find trust and peace in the midst of that because per usual, I journaled about it. I was not (because I could not) looking for my security in my bank account, or my retirement fund, or my job but only in Him. How many of us (especially Americans) can say that we feel secure in God when there is not a lot of money? There is story after story of the ways God provided us. One time in particular while Brad was at Mercer University finishing his degree, a random refund from the school came in and was over $1400. We were blown away! It was always just enough to cover whatever we needed. Don't get it twisted though, there were still times that my fickle heart wondered if I should go back out there, go back to banking or go back to corporate America so I could make "x" amount of dollars but I knew I had to choose. I could find another job like that but it mean giving up my four day work week which meant giving up my extra time to work on the ministry and I knew that we could either be comfortable financially or we could pursue what God was calling us to do. We were faithful in the calling and God has certainly been faithful in return.

We have some friends that used to own a lake house on Lake Jackson, approximately 45-50 minutes from our front door. They let us use it like it was our own and for a season when we couldn't afford vacations, it was a sweet,

sweet grace gift. For several years we had gone to the lake during the kids' spring break weeks and we would play outside for hours on end, play board games in front of the big windows overlooking the water, ride the paddle boats, fish, float, and everything in between. It was always so good for our souls. I always felt so close to God there because everything was naturally slower. Wi-Fi was spotty at best and you only had your people, the kitchen, and time to tend to. I always journaled and read books there and it is no surprise that on the 2016 spring break lake trip, the Lord spoke so clearly to me. He revealed to me that it was time to leave the non-profit where I was employed because it was time to jump head long into our non-profit, Cross Roads Recovery. There had been a situation at work that I needed to talk to my boss about so we met at Panera one morning before work. She began asking me about my future plans because she hired me knowing that my intent was to learn from her and my end goal was to operate Cross Roads. As we talked it through, the answer was abundantly clear and we both knew it was time for me to take the plunge headfirst into Cross Roads. It was one of the most amazing things God has ever done. He clearly orchestrated the meeting and the timing of my exit. As we wrapped up that day, tears filled my eyes and tears filled my boss' eyes too, and I told her that I felt like the weight of the world had been lifted off my shoulders. I walked out of Panera feeling light as a feather. God was not pushing me but leading me to another big faith step where I would lean on Him and grow my trust muscles even more. God is a gentleman, he doesn't take our burdens but waits for us to hand them over and he doesn't always yell to us but sometimes it is a gentle whisper and we have to turn down all the other noise in our life to hear it.

CHAPTER 30

Our New Gig

On May 5, 2016, my journal shows that it was my fourth day in my new gig at Cross Road. I wrote how much I loved it and how I was in my element. My Jesus Calling that day read "Relax in the knowledge that the one who controls your life is totally trustworthy. Come to me with confident expectations. There is nothing you need that I cannot provide."

Once again, don't get it twisted. I was not perfect and it was not always peaches and rainbows when I went full time at Cross Roads. I worked full time with my husband who is incredible but if you have ever worked with a spouse then you know and if not, you can't fully understand. I was eating my meals with his man, sleeping in the bed with this man, starting a ministry and working in it every day with this man. It was a lot of my man no matter how fabulous he is. We were both so grateful but no matter how grateful you are, you can still wear on each other's nerves. We knew that the enemy would like nothing more than to bring us down because the potential impact of the ministry would be forfeited if we couldn't do it together.

So, we started with the one man and we continued to add one more and one more until we were in a house big enough to hold them all.

There was a time in that big new house when we got down to one resident. He eventually left too and we knew we needed to hit the pause button on the whole thing. We needed to take a breather to recoup, re-evaluate, and figure things out. It was trial and error and we never claimed to know it all, so maybe someone reading this has started something and things aren't going super well at the moment. It happens. Know that you can hit the pause button. That is why the button is there. During that pause period, God showed up, he spoke to us, and gave us clear discernment and wisdom about things that needed to change as we questioned everything we thought we knew. We did that for a couple of months – we accepted no new residents, we re-evaluated it all and it was just what we needed to do. Can you imagine what we were feeling? We thought we were in a place for growth so we rented a house three times the size of anything we'd had before and now it was empty! What had we done? Turns out, exactly what was needed and God blessed it.

Be encouraged to know that hustling and doing the work don't always look like we imagine it should, sometimes it means to be still. Be still and know that He is God. Do you think that the ministry house has been empty since? Absolutely not, we are always busting at the seams and as soon as one graduates, a new fella is on the side lines waiting to come in and take that place. This is not our work, but the Lord's and it has been so evident that His hand has been in it all along.

During that time when the house was empty, my husband will be the first to tell you that God humbled him. He realized that God had called him to something that statistically he would never be good at. He always shares the story about the last guy leaving and him hitting his knees in his office asking God if he had misunderstood the calling. He was asking, "God, I know I was called but maybe it was to do something else related to addiction?" But God said, "Son, it is not working because YOU are trying to do it. You can't change a man's heart, only I can." In that moment Brad realized that he was just the man planting the seeds and God was the one who had to make them grow.

Mike Harden is a huge mentor to us and happens to be the founder of No Longer Bound. Mike started NLB 30 or so years ago and we are standing on his shoulders as we do this work and run our program modeled after his program. It was during that pause period that Mike gave Brad the best advice. He said, "You can't take credit for the good or the bad. If the negatives are affecting you greatly then you still have your arms wrapped around the positives in some way." BOOM. Mic drop. I mean it feels good to help people right? But we can't let our chests get puffy as we do the work because it is not us, it's God. You can't take credit for the good choices they make or the bad. I think that same advice can work for parenting too.

The other thing that happened in May of 2016 was Brad's college graduation. There was only about a 20 year gap between when he started and when he finished and that made his graduation day all the more glorious. Brad graduated with straight A's from the Penfield School of Mercer University on May 14, 2016. His degree is in Human Services with a concentration in Communication. You may remember that one of the first rehab programs Brad attended was named Penfield. It was in Union Point, Georgia and happens to be the original campus of Mercer University. We always laugh and say that he graduated from Penfield twice. Once from Penfield Addiction Recovery and once from the Penfield School of Mercer University. I imagine the people on that list is few and far between. To us it is more proof that God is in the details of our lives and that He has as sense of humor.

CHAPTER 31
God knows you by name

It is so cool to me to think that when God created Brad and when he created me that he ultimately knew this is where we would be. He knew the heartache and loss that would have to come, he knew the icky parts of the middle and He knows our final destination. I mentioned that back when Brad was in treatment, I referred to the friend (another wife known as AP in this book) that I made at NLB as my war buddy. The things you go through in a program of that kind of intensity reminds me of the bond you would form with someone that you really went off to war and fought with in a place like Vietnam or Iraq. Brad feels the same way about his brothers from NLB. We were not physically fighting but man did we fight spiritually, mentally, and emotionally.

Brad and I were walking around our neighborhood one day, years post treatment, and I made the comment that Brad would have been a good military man. He is naturally athletic and strong and is a faithful member of a workout group that was started by a Green Beret. They plant a flag before every workout, they speak in military lingo, regularly do endurance tests, and the flag is part of their logo. As we talked about that, Brad shared a memory with me from first grade. He said his teacher was teaching history, talking about the different roles of military officers. A General is defined as someone who has the title and rank of a senior army officer, one who commands large units, and who plans field operations. He is the guy you trust beyond measure and everyone feels safer when he is around. After that explanation one kid in class raised his hand and said "Brad Sappe would be a good General." I agree kid, I agree. He is in a war alright just not one with guns and ammo. He is fighting in the spiritual realm as He daily leads and coaches men out of the trenches of addiction and into the beautiful fields of recovery. He is a warrior and a mighty weapon for the Kingdom. Thank you, Jesus for saving him and in turn using him to save so many others.

One of my favorite quotes is by the legendary Walt Disney. He said, "Around here we don't look backwards for very long." We knew that to take on this ministry we had to have faith, courage, and ingenuity. We knew we would fail sometimes, and we would falter sometimes but we also knew we were called so that meant God would prepare us and equip us. We believed in our vision and we trusted a God that we had seen move mountains. We felt like a little like pioneers and if we'd had Davy Crockett hats we would have been all set. Things were rolling along in the ministry and we were in our second full year but only had one year of events under our belts. In the non-profit world you put on multiple events each year to raise funds for the work. We hosted an annual golf tournament and clay shoot the first two years and then added a Daddy Daughter event and some charity days with local boutiques along with a benefit we call the Blue Jean Ball. Things were busy and usually stressful.

In May of 2017 just before Mother's Day I started having some weird symptoms. On May 13th (the day before Mother's Day that year) I went to the salon to have my hair cut and colored. I wanted to be a vivacious red so I had chosen a fiery hue that I couldn't wait to get on my locks. I felt a little light headed in the two weeks leading up to this and had some numbness in my mouth but nothing too bad. I just attributed the light headed feeing to dehydration since I worked out every morning in the heat and probably didn't drink enough water. When I got ready to go to the salon that day, I thought my face looked a little funny but I went on and got my hair done like any good Southern woman would do. When I got back home early that afternoon, my husband looked at me and said, "Your hair looks great but something is wrong with your face." He is not subtle at all. I went and took a peek in the mirror and my mouth was crooked like something was wrong with one side of my face. Brad stayed back with the kids and I went to the ER just a few blocks from our house. They immediately took me back and started a stroke assessment. I didn't have slurred speech or weakness in my body so I felt pretty sure I wasn't having a stroke but it was scary nonetheless. It never failed that any time I ended up at the ER a guy we know always seemed to be working during my emergencies. On this particular day, it was such a relief to see him. They did tests and blood work and checked me out thoroughly and told me I did not have a stroke but that I was suffering from Bell's Palsy. The appearance of it is similar to what a stroke can cause because there is facial paralysis. I had heard of it but didn't know much about it. The doctors were encouraging and never mentioned to me that it might be permanent. They told me it would run its course and likely go away but there is no treatment and there is no particular time frame, it could last for three days or three months. I had honestly always had a fear of something happening to my face – some sort of sickness or injury that makeup couldn't cover up. But then it happened and it wasn't the end of the world. My perspective immediately shifted to one of thanks because I knew it could have been so much worse and in the grand scheme of life this wasn't a big deal. If nothing else, hard times give your perspective for sure.

I was probably able to more readily adopt the thankful point of view because as far as I knew it was temporary. It did end up being temporary for me as it lasted for roughly three weeks and my face went back to normal. I didn't learn until then that for some people it never goes away. I think the Lord protected me from knowing that because I truly embraced it while I was in it asking the Lord to reveal what He wanted to teach me and I might not have been such an eager student if I knew my face was changing forever. He taught me so much about vanity during that short season. I certainly don't have it whipped but I learned a lot. I kept living and didn't even stop taking pics or showing up just because I looked different. Since it all happened over Mother's Day weekend there is a picture of me and the kids at church in front of a photo wall and it is one of my favorite pics, crooked face and all. I even met and took a pic with one of my all time favorite singer/songwriters Mac Powell in that condition and it is another favorite picture. These pictures serve as reminders to me that we never know what the future holds but we know who holds the future and that is enough.

Mac Powell concert

Brad, Mac Powell, and Me

Our sweet friends, Dave & Emily

You can always find a reason to laugh and my trip to hospital on Mother's day weekend is no exception. When I was released that day, my regular pharmacy just down the street didn't have the medicine I needed so I had to drive a little a little farther to pick it up and on the way back home I got pulled over for speeding. I couldn't believe it. Could this day get any nuttier? The cop let me off with a warning and to this day I swear it was because of my bright red hair and the hospital bracelet. He probably thought this lady possibly just escaped from the psych ward so I am gonna go on and let her go. I have been a red head ever since.

CHAPTER 32

Onward

People often ask me what piece of advice I would give to someone who finds herself in a relationship with an addict. It is the same piece of advice that I give anyone who is in distress and that is to just cry out to Jesus. He can handle it and in His sovereignty, He is not caught off guard by the events of our lives. When I say cry out to Jesus, I mean just that. Sometimes you might not even have the words to pray, so just call His name. There is power in the name of Jesus. I even taught my kids this lesson. It drives them nuts but ever since they were little, if they fought or acted the fool, I would just call out the name of Jesus in the midst of it all. They would beg me to stop at first, then just roll their eyes and sometimes we'd end up laughing because not every situation required a Jesus summon but I was still teaching them to cry out when they needed Him. In all seriousness though, I would say cry out to Him as much and as often as you need to. Take care of yourself so that you can then effectively care for those around you and pray for wisdom and discernment. God will show you the way. He promises to always be with us and if we are walking towards Him, He will always meet us halfway.

The other question I get asked the most is about our kids and what it was like for them as a 4 and 7-year-old. You heard a little from their mouths in a previous chapter and their Dad had been to rehab before but this year long experience was the first time they needed an explanation. Addiction is a hard thing to explain and especially to children. So, I took a page from the book of a friend whose husband had recently gone to rehab. She told her seven-year-old son that Daddy had an allergy and he had gone to get some help so that is what I told my kids too. I told them he was allergic to some medicine and it made him sick. I said he was at a place that was going to help him get well and he would learn how to be the best Daddy and husband he could be. You hear it all the time but it is not just a cliché, kids are truly resilient. My kids were fine while Brad was away and then when we got visits, they thought they were living their best lives! Because of our journey, the kids were exposed to real life at an early age meaning they learned earlier than most that life is hard and there are consequences for our decisions. I made the decision early on to always be as transparent as possible with them, so I let them see my emotion and I have loved watching who they have become as a result. They are loving and open minded and they see people differently than most their age. They love the men in our program and are so proud of their Dad. Lawson will tell you that our residents are his best friends. He knows what it is like to be a little different, so he adores them. One Easter, the local paper did an article about our story and the ministry and that article obviously talked openly about drugs and rehab but all Lawson knew was that he was so proud of his Daddy for being in the paper so he cut out that article and took it to school in his backpack. We asked hm if any of the kids said anything about the article and he said one little boy said, "Your dad did drugs?" and Law told him that his Daddy made a bad choice but then he went and got help and now he helps other men. Well said Law dawg, well said.

That reminds me of a Facebook post that pops up in my memories from time to time. It was right after Law's baptism in March of 2013. I asked him how he felt afterwards and he said, "Mom, I feel like a real good changed man."

That is the best we can ever hope to be when Jesus lives in our hearts.

I love the story of Ruth because the story of Ruth reminds me that God does not seek perfection. He seeks those who come to him with a humble heart. He is really just asking us for small steps of obedience. Much like my story, in the beginning of Ruth's story, she had lost everything but then God stepped in and redeemed it all. There are a few books that have changed my life and one of them is the *Circle Maker* by Mark Batterson. I have not read a book by him that I have not loved but *Circle Maker* was a game changer for my prayer life.

Along the years of our ministry, there were a couple of opportunities for me to work outside of the ministry and each time an opportunity presented itself, I did my part to follow through and see what the Lord for me, always trusting that He would either open or close doors. Each time a new opportunity came, God ultimately always shut the door so I understood where I was supposed to be and what I was supposed to be doing – Cross Roads work. God has gotten even more specific over the years and towards the end of 2017 I knew He was calling me to go to graduate school and get my masters degree in counseling. I had been counseling for years as I had endless meetings with family members of addicts but in 2017 God began sending me all kinds of people, people that were dealing with things way out of my comfort zone. Things I knew nothing about so I prayed for clarity and God kept sending the people so I knew He wanted to get credentials. I set up a meeting with my personal counselor, Dr. Beers to tell him that I wanted to be a counselor. He asked me why and I answered that I thought I was being called because of all these people God was sending my way and it was no longer in familiar problem areas. He clapped his hands, laughed and said, "That's the right answer! You are clearly being called!" But then he didn't leave me hanging, he explained this his office, NPCC has a separate leg that they refer to as "The Academy" and I could essentially choose the school I wanted to attend and then study under Dr. Beers. It almost seemed too easy (until my first text book arrived) but I knew it was a divine appointment and a part of the Lord's plan for my life. I got to work and 2.5 years later in the Spring of 2020, I graduated Magna Cum Laude from Colorado Theological Seminary! Now, I have the honor and privilege of being the staff counselor for Cross Roads residents and the families and I also get to serve others in need through my private practice, J. Sappe Christian Counseling.

Life is funny like that, if you had asked me when I was nine years old or even 20 years old what I would be doing at 41, running a rehab and counseling would not have been my answer but I know this is exactly where I am supposed to be. To get to use what I have experienced plus what I have learned in school to help others is such an honor and I will never get over it.

I am so thankful for all the lessons I have learned along the way and one of the biggest is that God never wastes our pain. Even our darkest days have purpose because of who God is and who we are in Him. All of our days count.

They count for eternity. Live a life that counts friends. Leave a legacy and may you always be known for loving your people well.

CHAPTER 33

Brad Sappe

I talked a lot about Brad in this book and you heard from him a few times throughout, but I thought you might officially like to meet him. Keep reading to hear a little from my main man. I want to leave you with all my time favorite Brad quote:

"Some ships are built for smooth sailing. We ain't one of em'."

Hey everybody,

I am the guy you have been reading about. I am the infamous Brad, Jodi's husband. Thank you for taking the time to read this book. I hope that it has impacted you in some way and encouraged you in your walk with Christ. My wife is amazing but if you know her or read this book then you already know that. Without her, there is no story of us. Each time I am asked to speak, I always tell the audience that if they want to hear a really, good story, they need to talk to Jodi.

When Jodi dropped me off at NLB, I had no idea what God had in store for me. I thought I was going to perform my way through another rehab and it would be the same old song and dance. Nothing could have been further from the truth. I surrendered while in that program and God not only put me back together, He put my family back together.

When I started that program, everything in me wanted to call Jodi or walk off campus and get to her somehow so I could tell her my side of the story, make her feel sorry for me and manipulate my way back in but I knew I had done that far too many times only to continue to hurt her and eventually fail. I will never forget praying and saying, "God, if she comes back, it will have to be you that does it, not me. But no matter what I want you to be enough in my life. Not her, not my kids, not my job, but you."

I can remember being out in the NLB van one day doing some work in town and I had to stop for gas. I saw a Wells Fargo branch and wondered if Jodi was still paying the mortgage or if she had skipped town and burned all my clothes. Thankfully, she did pay the mortgage and she didn't burn my clothes.

There was a time when I never thought I would be free from addiction. I had come to terms with the fact that I would struggle for the rest of my life. The problem was that I kept looking at *what* I was doing instead of looking at *why* I was doing it. I knew for a long time that I couldn't "successfully" drink or use drugs. I knew that every time I started, I couldn't stop but I had never looked at the deeper issue of why I started using in the first place. That is why I love the idea of regeneration instead of rehabilitation. To rehabilitate is to return to a former state. Who I was when I started using is why I started using. I knew that I was angry about my Dad's death and I felt like I was just wasted potential. I was convinced that if certain things had not happened to me and if other people treated me the way I wanted to be treated then everything would be okay. I know now that nothing could be farther from the truth.

Everyone experiences hurt, everyone experiences pain, and people don't often treat us the way we want to be treated. We spend so much time focusing on the pain that we miss all the blessings. The good news is that we can be okay no matter what! That is what regeneration allows. Regeneration is to be regenerated or made new. I am now a new creation in Christ, the old has gone and the new has come. I heard my whole life that you reap what you sow. The problem with that is that many of us don't know how to sow anything worth reaping. We stay angry, bitter, and sad over small things that don't amount to much in the big picture. I know that God sees the big picture and he is more concerned with where I am headed than where I am currently sitting.

I never thought a real, personal relationship with God was possible for someone like me. In my young mind, God was a mythical creature who punished me when I did something wrong and expected me to be perfect. I spent my whole life trying to perform for love and acceptance never realizing that I was already loved and accepted beyond measure. God created me just the way he wanted me to be. Instead of trying to fit in and be liked, I can now walk in confidence knowing who I am and whose I am. I always say that I am fortunate to have had a problem with drugs and alcohol because people looked at me and said, "You need help," but they had no idea that using drugs was just a symptom of a much deeper problem. We all have problems and we deal with those problems in different ways. We don't feel accepted, we don't feel loved, we feel hurt, and we feel anger. Had I turned to work, social acceptance, money, eating, shopping, or a number of other things people do to numb the pain, society would have been less likely to tell me that I needed help. I am forever thankful that my problem led me to a place where I could get help and find freedom. For so long, I tried to get my love, acceptance, and worth from everything this world had to offer, and I finally realized it would never be enough. The good news is that God can and will always be enough!

We could fill lots more pages with all the stories associated with running a recovery ministry. Some would make you laugh, some would make you cheer, and some would break your heart. Nowadays, I often tell Jodi that I couldn't do this ministry work without her, some days I don't even know if I can do it with her but I know for sure that I couldn't do it without her.

Stay tuned. That sounds like a pretty good title for her next book to me.

2012 Family Pics- shortly before it all fell apart (Lawson 7, Bella 4)

Brad's first Thanksgiving post NLB- November 2014

Easter 2015

Brad with his mom on graduation day – Mercer University 2016

Family Beach Trip 2016
(left to right: Sister's husband, Sister, Mom, Dad, Me, Brad, Bella, & Lawson)

Easter 2017

17th Anniversary 2019

Me and Katherine

Bethany and Me

One of our first events for Cross Roads

Vicki and Charles

ACKNOWLEDGEMENTS

First, I want to recognize my parents, my sister, and my grandmother because I certainly would not have survived any of this without their constant love and support. They were steady and faithful to my little family & they faithfully prayed for Brad.

Vicki & Charles, you are the salt of the earth. We pray that all you have poured out in your lives will be returned to you ten-fold. It is safe to say that you two will have the shiniest mansion in the sky.

Dr. Beers, you were the vessel that God used to get us to No Longer Bound and that in turn was the vessel that saved Brad, saved our marriage, and our family. Your gifts were also used to save me during the hardest days. Forever grateful for you and you work.

I want to thank all of my dearest friends for being there not just through this journey but through so many life events. The friends I grew up with, my High School crew, my college buddies, and the people I met early in my marriage. You have been the hands and feet of Jesus in my life.

I want to thank my mother-in- law for her love and prayers. And also, for the way she nourishes our stomachs and souls with her home cooked food.

Gannie Faye & Pop Pop, thank you for your unconditional love and prayers.

Law & Bella, thank you for being you. I can't wait to see what God has in store for each of your lives!

Thank you, Mike Hardin for following you heart and opening No Longer Bound. Thousands of lives have been saved and generations of families are healthy because of your vision and work.

To NLB, thank you for the work you do day in and day out. You are difference makers. 2725 Pine Grove Road will always be sacred ground to our family.

To the families of the Cross Roads residents, thank you for entrusting your loved ones to us for a little while.

And last but not least, Brad, this book would not have been written without you. I don't know if that is a good thing or a bad thing ☺ You are a star character in my life and have kept me laughing almost always. Your heart, drive, and leadership inspire me daily & I will never be able to fully thank God for what He has done in your life. Your wisdom and discernment are beyond compare and that is such a gift. Thank you for doing the hard things and doing whatever it took to get back to us. You are dearly loved.

"Now to him who is able to do immeasurably more than all we ask or imagine, according to his power that is at work within us." Ephesians 3:20